The CAPEX Formula for Learning & Performance

How to Gain Competitive Advantage by Harnessing New Technology and Developing Your Workforce

KEVIN McALPIN & DANI SAADU

The CAPEX formula for Learning and Performance

First published in Great Britain in October 2023 by Rock-Hill Publishing

Rock-Hill Publishing
Central House
4 Roborough Walk
Hornchurch
Essex
RM126QJ

First Edition 2023
British Library Cataloguing in publication Data
A catalogue record for this book is available from the British Library

Print Edition ISBN: 978-1-7395753-0-4
Ebook edition ISBN: 978-1-7395753-1-1

CONTENTS

ACKNOWLEDGEMENTS

We would like to dedicate this book to all our friends, colleagues and the clients of Performance Coaching International. We have learnt so much from them in the writing of this book, and thank each one for their insights, experiences, hard work, time, feedback, and belief. This book wouldn't have been possible without the help of:

Ali McBride
Ali Mohammed
Alistair Cumming
Ann Akers
Bertie Tonks
Beverley McMaster
Carl Rayne
Cathy Strachan
Ceri James
Chris Oakes
Cora-Lynn Heimer Rathbone
Damian Holt
David Norrington
David Picton
Edward Gordon-Lennox
Emma Wright
Ewa Francis
Graham Herbert
Ingo Perizonius
Jamie Tott
Jay Muthu
Jeff Weigh
Jo Drury
Krushma Makwana
Leena Nair
Lisa Cherry
Lucy Hope
Mark Edgerton
Mark Griffiths
Mark Latteman
Martin Whitehouse
Matt Burton
Melanie Hayes
Michael Millar
Nicholas McAlpin
Paul Matthews
Perry Timms
Peter Cheese

Peter Collyer
Ray Mulvey
Robert Ashcroft
Simon Haben
Steve Harvey
Tracey Elston
Tracey Harman
Trevor Hoyle
Vidya Krishnan
Will Carnegie

Dani would like to dedicate this book to his Dad, who died of coronavirus on Tuesday, 31st March 2020. His father, Dr Alfa Saadu, was the 4th doctor to die of COVID-19 in the UK, and it made the national news. His father worked for the NHS his whole career and then part-time for a memorial hospital until his death. His father's legacy and recognition of service to the NHS is the primary driver to pushing Dani out of his comfort zone and getting him to write this book with Kevin after many years of encouragement.

ABOUT THE AUTHORS

KEVIN MCALPIN

Kevin is an award-winning learning innovator, global executive coach, and founder of Performance Coaching International.

For more than 20 years, he has successfully delivered strategies and tactics designed to change how people think, feel and behave in the workplace, consistently improving careers, corporate cultures, and business returns.

He has worked with a vast range of organisations, from FTSE 100 and Fortune 500 companies, to governments across Europe, Africa, Asia, the Middle East, North America and Oceania. This long experience gives him a unique insight into human resources, learning cultures, and building world class performance.

Kevin has held various HR board level and non-executive director roles. He regularly speaks at conferences and appears in the media as a thought leader in the field of leadership and learning.

DANI SAADU

Dani is Head of People and Culture at Wavemaker UK. He has a proven track record in developing and delivering global people programmes and frameworks.

Dani is a certified Scrum Master and Lean Six Sigma specialist with a focus on ensuring that people and culture concepts are translated into practical and sustainable deliverables that provide measurable returns on investment.

Dani specialises in HR and operational excellence, talent management, change management, and organisational development. He is known as an innovator, conference speaker, and thought leader in the field of learning and performance.

He has held people development roles in a range of sectors, including pharmaceuticals, retail, recruitment, healthcare, and travel. His experience spans senior leadership roles across the EMEA, Americas, and Asia Pacific regions.

A NOTE FROM KEVIN & DANI

We have known each other and worked together over many years, but the CAPEX formula marks our first collaboration in print. This book is a testament to how different skills, experiences, and perspectives can be brought together to become greater than the sum of their parts.

This book integrates the worlds of external consultancy and corporate HR, OD and learning, giving you the full story. It brings Kevin's insights from world-leading brands together with Dani's experience with younger, more agile, and innovative organisations that are disrupting their markets and transforming how we do business.

It balances a down-to-earth, practical business approach with psychological understanding. It blends Dani's passion for technology, AI, and the future of work, with Kevin's expertise in the areas of organisational culture, purpose, and behavioural change. Dani's experience in creating inclusive cultures and harnessing diversity squares neatly with Kevin's focus on strategic thinking and his insight into the trends and patterns that drive innovation.

But at the heart of our ground-breaking CAPEX formula lies a shared passion for the kind of learning, leadership, and performance management that will be crucial for people and companies to thrive in the future of work. It is a collaboration built on a long friendship that is, itself, founded on a passion for making a difference to people, organisations, and the world of work.

We hope it will change the way you look at workforce development in a rapidly changing world.

Kevin & Dani

4IR – WHAT'S THE BIG DEAL?

We have worked with some of the world's leading brands, multinational companies and disruptive innovators since the 1990s. We have focused on Leadership, Organisational Development (OD), Learning and Development (L&D) and Human Resources (HR). We have seen strategies and tactics shift and evolve, and seen fads come and go. But we haven't ever seen change of the magnitude that is with us now. It is a time of extraordinary upheaval… and enormous potential.

Notions of 'sea changes' and 'paradigm shifts' have been thrown around for so long by leaders and management consultants as to become almost meaningless. But the new world of work, encompassing the Fourth Industrial Revolution (4IR) – or Industry 4.0 as it is also known – is the real deal. It is already changing the way we live, consume, work, and do business. And, for the avoidance of doubt, it is not coming soon, it is already here! As it progresses, the velocity, scope, systems, and impact of change will be unlike anything we've seen before.

The focus of this new era is all too often seen as disruptive technology, such as Artificial Intelligence (AI), the Internet of Things (IoT), robotics and Virtual Reality (VR). These innovations offer real opportunities (or threats, depending on your point of view). Most business leaders are now using or at least aware of these technologies, but they are unclear as to how they can rewire their organisation and effectively integrate the systems, processes, and people to maximise their value to the organisation. They are often considered better left to the 'tech' professionals. The narrative around harnessing them is often incomplete as it stresses what the tech can do, but ignores one indispensable ingredient. And that ingredient will be crucial to distinguishing the organisations that embrace the new world of work successfully from those that are left behind. That ingredient is human beings, and their ability to learn and adapt in this ever-shifting environment.

IT IS NOT *TECH* AT THE EXPENSE OF *PEOPLE*

The problem we see time and again is companies investing heavily in technology to ride the oncoming wave, while forgetting that it is the people in the organisation and their ability to learn that will ensure the company's success. It is the drive, creativity, and expertise of a company's workforce that ensures technology is deployed to its maximum potential. While new technology generally becomes more widely available to everyone in some form over time, that is simply not the case when it comes to people. As the Fourth Industrial Revolution progresses, *talented people* will be even more valuable than smart tech. This will be the true differentiator in business success. How firms access and leverage that talent will determine winners and losers.

While many fear that the technology replaces people, in a smart organisation it enhances their performance. Someone after all must be at the controls, and if they don't know what they are doing the whole thing will either stall or pull itself apart.

If we put people centre stage it follows that in a time of such rapid innovation and change the spotlight must fall on their learning and skills. The most innovative firms are not asking how they can outperform their opposition. They are asking how they can outlearn them. Any business wanting to remain relevant needs to have a culture of continuous learning. Such a culture drives innovation, but it also drives talent acquisition and loyalty as you become a more attractive environment to be in.

The increasing importance and constant, rapid evolution of technology means we are locked in a high-speed learning cycle, which will require constant reskilling and upskilling. Diane Gherson, Senior VP and former Chief Human Resources Officer at IBM, laid this out starkly when she explained the shelf life of skills in technology. She believes only 50% of the information learnt five years ago remains relevant today and in some areas it is redundant after just three years. Research for the World Economic Forum (WEF) found two out of three employers expect to see a return on investment (ROI) from their reskilling activities within one year. This demonstrates a sense of urgency in building the right skills for the future, as well as a fear of obsolescence if skills aren't updated.[1]

Research from PriceWaterhouseCoopers (PwC) showed 80% of Chief Executive Officers (CEOs) worried about the skills gap in their firms.[2] Another report by the IBM Institute for Business Value (which includes input from more than 5,670 global executives in 48 countries) showed the issue is getting more acute, with the time it takes to close a skills gap increasing by more than tenfold. In 2014, it took an individual three days (on average) to learn what was needed to close a capability gap. In 2018, this rose to 36 days.[3] Taken with the previous data, we could be requiring our people to spend 12 days a year over three years to reskill now, as opposed to a couple of days per year over five years. And remember, these results come from 2018. The new hybrid world of work is here and there are new skills to be learnt by many. That training and development requirement can only have increased as we've adapted to the technological revolution.

Focusing on employee learning as the key differentiator of success brings many challenges. As the saying goes, 'people are a lot more complicated than machines'. They are also harder to manage and inspire. The tech you invest in might seem indescribably complex, work in ways you never fully understand, and execute its tasks at speeds that are mind-blowing. But tech doesn't expect to be given a sense of purpose; it won't demand that it be part of an inclusive community; or expect you to balance making profits with your duty to protect the planet.

Machines might seem easier to deal with than people but you ignore them and their fundamental needs at your peril. Instead you must embrace the notion of a close working relationship between people and technology, where each brings crucially different skills to the table. Skills that, in the case of people, need to be nurtured, honed, and crafted in a way that can't be done from a system upgrade or reboot. Skills that can be put to work to achieve amazing things, but also can easily be withheld for many reasons.

LEARNING IS EVOLVING TOO

We live in a world where leaders are increasingly managing people and machines simultaneously. The best way to facilitate this balance is through learning – a discipline that is evolving almost as fast the technology itself. Over the past few years, neuroscientists, cognitive psychologists and behavioural change experts have achieved major breakthroughs in their understanding of how people learn and adapt, as well as what motivates, engages and inspires people.[4] We will look at all these new approaches and how you can leverage them in an era that, in the often-quoted words of Peter Hinssen, is no longer the 'new normal', but has now become the 'never normal'.[5]

And let us be clear: we are not just talking about developing critical digital and technological skills (which has been so much the focus of corporate learning of late). We're talking about individuals and whole organisations needing to learn how to develop and nurture a culture of productivity, positivity, wellbeing, resilience, happiness and trust – where people feel they *belong* if they are to deliver high performance in return.

We will also need to teach new ways of thinking that encourage insight-driven decisions and release a torrent of creativity and innovation. We will need to understand and learn how to adapt and change behaviour to suit rapidly changing environments and scenarios.

This list of demands goes on and on, but at its core lies a simple message: *success will only be achieved through learning*. It won't be easy, but organisations that accept and adopt this approach will survive and thrive.

FUTURE-PROOFING YOUR ORGANISATION

For many organisations a central commitment to employee learning will need a refocus. For others the idea that learning can drive performance, as much as technology, or increasing sales, or driving down costs, will be new. This book is a guide for anyone who is interested in future-proofing their organisation as well as those working in learning and development. Business owners, boards and management teams must embrace and direct this change, while Chief Learning Officers, Heads of Learning and Development, Chief Human Resources Officers, Human Resources Directors (or anyone else who works in talent and leadership development, employee engagement, or HR business partner capacity) will be the ones to implement it.

ORGANISATIONAL LEARNING & DEVELOPMENT (OL&D)

In many organisations, employee learning is a standalone function. In others, it is part of the wider people-management function, which has many names: Human Resources, People and Culture, Personnel… the list goes on. No doubt that label will change again as much of the work currently delivered by this department is in the process of being automated. Many of the tasks that firms rely on HR departments for – and which take up a lot of the energy and focus of their teams – will soon become functional, business-as-usual activities that algorithms will happily manage. Real value will come from a change of focus to Organisational Learning (OL) and Organisational Development (OD).

OL itself has many names, including 'corporate learning', and you might hear it described in the context of creating a 'learning culture', 'learning environment' or 'learning organisation', as first described by Peter Senge is his book *The Fifth Discipline*. Let us be clear about what this jargon means:

> *The process by which an organisation improves itself over time through gaining real time experience, creating and transferring knowledge, and enabling behaviour change.*

This is often coupled with 'organisational development', which the Chartered Institute of Personnel and Development (CIPD) defines as:

> *The planned and systematic approach to enabling sustained organisation performance through the involvement of its people.*[6]

These two disciplines are the future of the people profession and the focus of this book. They are inextricably linked and for that reason we refer to them as a single entity: Organisational Learning & Development (OL&D). When combined and executed well, these elements can be enormously powerful. They can maximise performance and create the cultural bedrock needed to build and sustain an organisation. But they also need to become the definition and guiding mission of what corporate learning needs to become and to deliver. This is a much wider remit than most learning professionals expect, but it can't stay that way.

Now, let us talk about timing. There's a lot of experimentation going on at the moment, with organisations trying to work out which technology works for their business. This begs the question as to whether you should be thinking in 4IR terms yet, particularly if you don't have the money to invest in tech or if such developments still feel years away in your industry or business.

Remember, thinking that 4IR is 'future technology' is a mistake. Regardless of where you are on your journey towards the future, the real difference isn't in the technology. The real difference will be people and their ability to learn in an environment shaped by their wider experience of 4IR. Whether you adopt 4IR technology yet or not, your people are already experiencing it in their lives outside of the workplace. And if that's the case, they may be wondering why you aren't keeping pace.

It may be more appealing to some employees to work where exciting new technology is being embraced.

Rather than focusing on tech first, business leaders should be devoting time to activities that:

- add the most value
- transform performance.

TALKING THE LANGUAGE OF BUSINESS

Data and analytics allow People and Culture experts to talk the language of business and demonstrate their value like never before. Macro data and internal information can be harnessed to clearly show the importance of upskilling a workforce in terms of the direct impact on the bottom line of the business. It can allow us to directly show the business value and return on investment. Data and analytics have become learning and HR professionals' best friend.

For a long time, this was not the case. Perhaps that's why profit and loss statements classify people only as a cost, and not as an asset. Surely in the 21st century this should not be the case. You can truly reposition employees – and that includes yourself – as an asset.

The radical changes 4IR brings, and the ability to measure output more easily means that, perhaps for the first time, businesses truly *need* learning professionals. The function is no longer a regulatory necessity, or an employee benefit to boost talent acquisition or staff retention. It correlates directly with improved performance. It is a strategic necessity.

This marks a radical change. The perception that those delivering Learning and People Strategy are a support function has long been driven by an inability to prove value (however intuitive results might have been, they lacked convincing numbers to back them up). Forward-looking leaders cannot escape the truth that their workforce is going to have to be constantly upskilling and reskilling to stay relevant, let alone get ahead.

THE RISE OF A NEW LEARNING CULTURE

The new world we inhabit, has amplified the importance of good leadership, and highlighted poor leadership. It has brought into sharp relief the need for a new style of leadership that embraces flexibility and adaptability. Those who do not learn and adapt are already being left behind or going under. There is more of this reshaping to come.

The COVID-19 pandemic demonstrated the power and importance of learning. It is telling that LinkedIn's 2020 learning survey found 60% of respondents said the culture of learning in their organisation had increased and become stronger during that period. This shock to the system forced most sectors to confront the fact that the ability to learn and adapt is crucial to an organisation's future wellbeing. *The Economist* went as far as likening the role played by human resource leaders and their learning and people strategies in the pandemic to that played by their financial counterparts during the global financial crisis:

> *When the financial crisis rocked the business world in 2007–09, boardrooms turned to corporate finance chiefs. A good CFO could save a company; a bad one might bury it. The COVID-19 pandemic presents a different challenge – and highlights the role of another corporate function, often unfairly dismissed as soft. Never before have more firms needed a hard-headed HR boss.*[7]

This recognition has been a very, very long time coming. It might have been more than 30 years since Jack Welsh created the world's first Chief Learning Officer (CLO) position (when he appointed Steve Kerr to the role at General Electric) but precious few companies have followed suit with similar executive-level roles. There are some notable exceptions: Facebook has a Global Head of L&D and Google has a Vice President of People Development and other firms bucking the trend are Merck and Citi. But there aren't nearly enough of these companies.

Things are changing. Progressive C-Suite (in other words, top-level) executives are focused on learning and building skills like never before. People are now at the front of their mind and learning has become a strategic financial driver of a business's future.

LESS TALK, MORE ACTION

This book offers a strategic focus, allowing you to concentrate on the five key priorities that will deliver the greatest ROI for your business. They are:

- Culture
- Adaptability
- Purpose
- Expectations
- X-Factor.

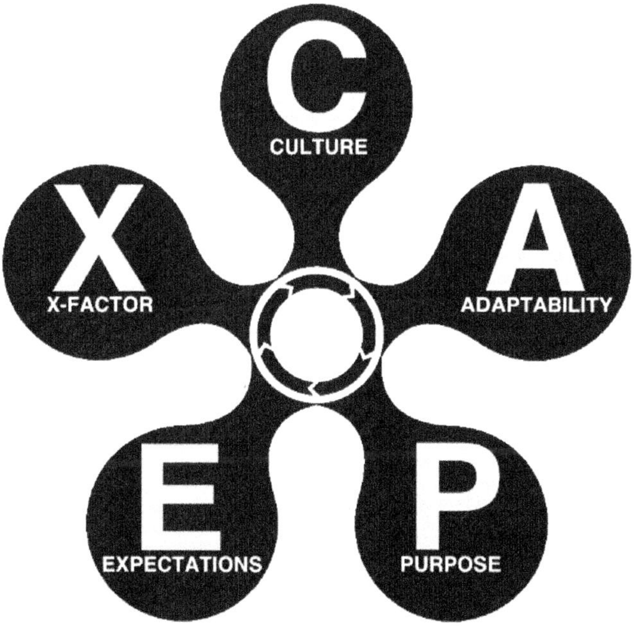

Delivering in these areas will help bring the most talented people to your organisation and keep them there. You will make an impact from the moment they first look at your company website and are engaged by its timely, relevant and engaging messages, through to the digital recruitment and selection process that offers greater scale, more inclusivity, and shorter time to hire.

It doesn't stop there. Your input will see your organisation serving your colleagues' needs and expectations in a way that boosts employee engagement and drives productivity higher. It will facilitate agility and innovation that will permeate through the organisation. It will drive clear, business-orientated results.

Strategies and tactics that use integrated organisational learning and development (OL&D) will help organisations grow and flourish. This approach has truly come of age and will drive the learning profession to become everything it can be, *aided* by technology that lets us be clear on priorities, automate manual activities, process vast amounts of data, and join up organisation-wide dots.

On our respective journeys, we have encountered firms that are great at this and others that are not. We have included some of these experiences – good and bad – so that you can learn from them. We have also met some of the most inspiring, creative, commercial, practical, and strategic individuals who have ripped up the playbook for their organisation's success. And make no mistake: your current playbook is going to have to go.

If you worry it is going to be tough to get your head around all this, then rest assured you are not alone. We have often run sessions for executives, learning professionals and HR leaders focused on transforming their corporate learning, so it is more meaningful to their business.

One exercise Kevin frequently runs in his coaching sessions is to give a team a single physical copy of his book on presentation skills, *Presenting the Penguin Way*. He then gives the team ten minutes to digest the contents of that single copy (which takes over an hour to read). Their task as a team is to verbally present a précis of the whole book after the allotted ten minutes. Each member of the team has to present for an equal amount of time. Cue lots of head scratching, tugging at the book, and mumblings about how it is impossible.

Eventually some (not many) realise the only way they can complete the task is to tear up the playbook: literally. This is the only way each person can have their own piece, digest it, and present it back successfully. But the idea of tearing up a book makes many people deeply uncomfortable. It goes against their beliefs and values (including ours). Almost without exception they display an ingrained belief that it is wrong to rip up the book; so much so, that for many participants it doesn't even register as an option, even when Kevin specifically asks them to display innovation and think differently. More than 75% of teams fail the task.

The point of the exercise is to show that traditional ways of thinking may no longer apply when a new challenge surfaces. We need to step outside our comfort zones; we need to challenge orthodoxies and ourselves.

It is crucial you realise you are not alone in taking on this challenge. You are not the first to face up to it, nor will you be the last. The important thing is to embrace the great changes that are coming and the many that are already here. Doing this will set you, and the organisations lucky enough to have you, apart and help you to thrive in this new era.

We have combined decades of personal experience with the collective intelligence of the innovative, inspiring freethinkers we have worked with. This book harnesses their ideas, strategies, and priorities for the new world of work, and combines them with our analysis of emerging trends, themes, and innovations to offer a fresh picture of the future.

The result of all this work is the CAPEX Formula. Not to be confused with the financial term 'capital expenditure', although the greatest capital in your business isn't cash anyway, it is your people. This formula explains the underlying drivers of effective learning in the new world of work and sets out clear steps you can implement in your own business.

We will demonstrate why and how learning professionals can become a strategic partner that shapes core elements of business thinking and behaviour, using concrete examples from some of the world's most innovative and successful organisations. You will learn how these learning pioneers have transformed their roles and output, driving tangible return on investment and making their respective organisations fit to flourish in this new era.

Specifically, we will look at:

- mega-trends driving the future of work
- priorities, research and analytics that are transforming corporate learning and directly impacting the bottom line
- the latest learning from pioneers
- innovations from 'agile' and 'design thinking'
- understanding behavioural change from the fields of neuroscience and psychology.

These insights will help ensure your organisation and people remain relevant, as well as help you be an employer of choice.

On the flipside, we won't duck the challenges that come with these opportunities. We will look at the current reality of the learning and development function in most organisations. Also, the trials faced by industry, leaders, and learning professionals alike.

The Fourth Industrial Revolution is upon us. It is not going away. A lot of organisations will be left behind – and a lot quicker than they expect. But it is a time of extraordinary opportunity for those who grasp it. As the novelist William Gibson said: 'The future is already here – it's just not very evenly distributed.'

THE DAWN OF A NEW ERA

THE PRECEDING INDUSTRIAL REVOLUTIONS

This is not a history book, but it is important to understand exactly how seismic the change we are living through is now. This is a truly pivotal moment in human history, where 'business as usual' simply doesn't apply. We aren't going back to how things used to be.

At each new stage in industrial development those organisations that could not, or would not, change went under. Look at the decline of what were once well-established industries to see this is true. There are no more coal-and-steam-powered cotton mills, and it would be ridiculous to propose a business model using this technology today. Who uses an overhead projector or telegraph anymore? Few people.

We are in a similar era now, where technologies of the recent past will very soon be obsolete. Embrace change and be a pioneer in the new ways of working. Stick your head in the sand and watch your business fail. Understand that even the word 'new' will be obsolete within years, or maybe months, and will be replaced by a new 'new'. Imagine business owners on the cusp of each revolution, struggling with the same issues we face today – adapt or die. What advice would you give them? *Adapt*, hopefully.

The First Industrial Revolution (1760–1820/40) saw the advent of mechanisation and the advent of steam and water power giving new meaning to horse-power. It incorporated the mass exploitation of coal as a fuel, and society shifted from an agricultural to an industrial one, with mass migrations of workers from the country to ever-growing towns and cities.

The Second Industrial Revolution (1871–1914), also known as the Technological Revolution, saw electricity emerge as a vital power source. This also saw the rise of other fossil fuels – gas and oil. Mechanisation of production lines saw mass-production of consumer goods and had military applications in the Great War.

The Third Industrial Revolution (late 20th century) or Digital Revolution, was the development of electronics, information technology, nuclear energy, space exploration, and further automation.

WHAT IS THE FOURTH INDUSTRIAL REVOLUTION (4IR)?

And now, here we are in the Fourth Industrial Revolution, where the boundaries between humans and machines starts to blur. Robotics, connectivity, artificial intelligence, cloud computing, autonomous devices, smart devices, Internet of Things, facial ID recognition, digital healthcare sensors, big data. And, although renewable energy has been around for centuries, it now has wider application and may, one day, replace fossil fuels as climate change becomes a driving force in societies around the world. Environmental issues seem ready to set technological and corporate agendas in a way that was virtually unheard of in the past.

- Procter & Gamble has committed to making all their materials either recyclable or reusable by 2030.
- Microsoft aims to be carbon neutral by 2030.
- Johnson and Johnson aims to procure 100% of their energy needs from renewable sources by 2050 (with various other milestones along the way).
- Google has committed over $1bn to renewable energy projects to enable other businesses to reduce their environmental impact through services such as Gmail.

- Coca-Cola has made major changes to its supply chain practices, including investing in new alternatively fuelled lorries, with the aim of creating a 25% reduction in their carbon footprint by 2030; setting an ambition to achieve net-zero by 2050.
- Bosch are focusing on environmental protection across their entire value chain. Their commitment is to reduce upstream and downstream emissions by 15% with a deadline of 2030.
- Lego has promised to invest $150m from 2015–30, with a focus on addressing climate change and reducing waste. It has reduced packaging, invested in alternative energy sources, and plans to make all Lego packaging from renewable and recyclable materials by 2025. Making all Lego bricks from sustainable sources by 2030.

We are in a time of fundamental change in the way we live, work and relate to one another.

Professor Klaus Schwab, executive chairman of the World Economic Forum (WEF), popularised the term the Fourth Industrial revolution, although it was created by a team of scientists in Germany.[8] It serves to highlight a series of social, political, cultural, and economic advancements impacting the physical, digital and biological worlds.[9]

This new era will build and extend the impact of digitisation on our lives and our environment in new and unanticipated ways. But this is more than just exciting new forms of digital delivery. WEF described it as 'the advent of cyber-physical systems involving entirely new capabilities for people and machines'.[10]

While WEF points out that these capabilities are reliant on the technologies and infrastructure of the Third Industrial Revolution (which brought the development of digital systems, communication and rapid advances in computing power), it is at pains to say this new era is so much more. 4IR represents entirely new ways in which technology becomes embedded within societies and even our bodies. In Schwab's words:

> *The speed of current breakthroughs has no historical precedent. When compared with previous industrial revolutions, the Fourth is evolving at an exponential rather than a linear pace. Moreover, it is disrupting almost every industry in every country.*[11]

Gerd Leonhard put it succinctly when he observed: 'Science fiction is now science fact.'[12]

THE URGENT NEED TO CHANGE AND ADAPT

We face some stark realities:

- It is already theoretically possible to automate around 50% of current work tasks.[13]
- The majority of the global workforce needs considerable training and development.[14]
- By 2035, 8.3m jobs will be lost in industry in Western Europe, against 10m new jobs created by market changes.[15]

Time is of the essence if your organisation wants to make the necessary transition to the new business landscape of 4IR. Historically, adapting to previous industrial revolutions took many years. Business and society tended to have ten or more years of confusion and uncertainty and, crucially, widespread adoption took time. Today, we do not have that luxury. 'Exponential' is an adjective that comes up again and again in the context of 4IR. Moreover, it is not a question of *if* you do this, rather, it is a question of *how well* you adapt to this new reality.

The good news is that many organisations have already proved remarkably adept at leveraging the benefits of 4IR. In 2020, Australia set up a nationwide telehealth service in record time. After completion of this extraordinary feat, the country's National Health Minister remarked that they had achieved 'a decade's worth of work in a matter of days'.[16] None of this would have been possible without the technological advancements of 4IR, and the people with the creativity to apply it.

This Australian example was born of pandemic necessity, but innovative organisations are looking at how they might harness this same mindset to achieve amazing things, because they realise this will soon become the standard way of working.

PEOPLE AND MACHINES

This new reality throws up a lot of challenges when it comes to managing the intersection between human beings and technology.

PRODUCTIVITY GAIN: BOOST OR BLUNDER?

Firstly, there is no point in getting humans to compete with machines to do the same job. Rather, to maximise the benefits that advances in technology are bringing, organisations must redesign jobs to focus on the human aspects of work. Machines cannot replace or replicate all things to our satisfaction, including: critical thinking, problem-solving, empathy, communication, judgement, decision-making and design. Although, in a few years' time we might revise this paragraph.

As such, jobs will not evaporate wholesale before our eyes, as breathless media stories so often report. Futurists tell us that there will just be different roles and responsibilities for humans to play: employees will be collaborating with robots, AI and machines in a complementary way. Traditional jobs will be reshaped, and new roles developed that do not exist today. Leadership will apply to both people and machines.

Before we leap to bemoan the end of humanity and the rise of the machines in some dystopian hysteria, let us consider the advances that have been made to the conditions for our workforces since the 18th century. While poverty still exists around the world, we do not have the same degree of abject misery in our society that was experienced by those too poor to survive. Gone are the workhouses (although only in the early twentieth century), and that is a result of progressive application of technology. Today's healthcare, for example, would be virtually unrecognisable to a citizen of even fifty years ago.

The challenge will be managing this next transition so we can move into a world of continuous learning, reskilling, growth and creativity. Doing all this requires a fundamentally different approach to work and learning.

With this in mind, let us look at productivity as a good example of how 4IR is changing our working practices. The arrival of a rapid Internet search capability and Chatbots using generative AI technology means we can access knowledge in seconds that would have taken hours or even days to find just a few years ago. With the speed at which we can access information getting faster, futurists predict that we will reach a tipping point where robotics, automation and digital assistants will take over much of our daily grind, meaning we might need to only work three-to-four hours per day to do the equivalent of a full day's work today.

If an organisation can learn and adapt to this it could reap huge benefits in terms of productivity and find an antidote to the current rise of *presenteeism* in the workplace. We must remember that being present for hours on end (even if appearing to be working hard) is different from productivity – it is the *quality* of output that matters.

This could be a major boost for companies and economies. According to data from the UK's Office for National Statistics and analysed by the Royal Statistical Society, between 2010–19, growth in productivity in the country slowed to a virtual standstill at an annual average of just 0.3%.[17] In fact, at the start of 2020 output per hour worked was nearly 2% lower than it was at the start of the recession in 2008. In 2022 it moved just above 2019 levels, which is far from optimal. If we follow the train of thought above, we could allocate certain tasks to machines, giving us more time to do high-value tasks and so increase productivity. It seems obvious, doesn't it?

Sadly, nothing is ever that easy. We have fallen into the trap of thinking of technology as a panacea and must instead return to that crucial, overlooked, and unpredictable element: people. We must not consider the benefits of technology outside of the human context.

What happens if we bring in this clever new tech and, rather than make things better, it brings uncertainty, confusion and mistrust? What if the much-heralded shiny machines and software damage the fabric of the relationship between colleagues and the organisation? What will happen to engagement and productivity? Learning, understanding, and the ability to adapt will be essential.

PERSONALISATION: SAVIOUR OR SCOURGE?

Another key development is personalisation. There is no better example of this than the use of data analytics to serve up bespoke products, services, and advertising. Treating people as individuals, and not as part of a group or segment, is one of the most important long-term trends in technology. Consumers have come to expect it and research shows personalisation is a great tool for building customer loyalty.

But let us look at another consequence of this advance, which organisations are going to have to face up to if they want to thrive in the future: the growth of the 'me culture'. We're talking about the impact that individualisation has on people's expectations, mental health, and wellbeing in the workplace.

Like many businesses, social media platforms (Facebook, Instagram, X, Google, WhatsApp, etc.) are specialists in personalisation. Users of these platforms are becoming conditioned by instant gratification, whether it be through real-time updates (like the scrolling ellipses when someone is typing a reply to your message, or live updates of sports scores), immediate responses and feedback (threads that become real-time conversations), or brain-changing affirmations (likes and shares). This environment creates an expectation for similar immediacy at work. And it has created serious mental health issues, which cannot be left at home when it is time to start the working day. Additionally, work-related social media can follow an employee home. Add remote and hybrid working into the mix and the lines of work-life balance are becoming ever more blurred.

Young professionals early in their careers are the most vulnerable. They are twice as likely to suffer from depression compared to the average employee. A Prince's Trust survey found 57% of people aged 16–25 thought social media created overwhelming pressure to somehow be perfect; a phenomenon that carries into the workplace.[18] Conversely, when they enter the world of work, they wonder where the instant feedback they've become used to has gone. They can become anxious and interpret silence as a sign that they are doing something wrong or are disliked. These people also regularly report feeling hyper-connected through technology, yet increasingly alone and isolated when it comes to human interaction.

Leaders must address issues like this. And if they can't be persuaded to do so based on the serious psychological impact this can have on human beings, then they will surely be moved by the obvious impacts on productivity, performance and their bottom line.

FLEXIBLE WORKFORCES: HEROES OR VILLAINS?

Not so long ago, the world of temporary contracts, freelance working, and 'gig' employment (completion of micro jobs, generally for small sums of money and without job security) used to be referred to as 'alternative work'. Now it is mainstream. Highly flexible jobs – that often come with high levels of insecurity – are now commonplace. The notion of a 'job for life' is an anachronism. Take just three global gig platforms – *Freelancer*, *Upwork* and *Zhubaji* – collectively they have over 60m users. That's a huge number of people looking for daily work through just three online platforms. And there are many, many more sites to choose from.

On one hand, this freelance way of working is held up as a symbol of the empowerment enjoyed by forward-thinking workers. The argument then goes that a gig economy provides more autonomy for someone to do the kind of work that they want to do, when they want to do it, and whomsoever they want to do it for.

On the other hand, independent contractors are often portrayed as victims of exploitation, working without benefits or employment rights, and being paid unsustainably low wages.

This is not a book on the ethics of the gig economy, but it appears to be here to stay as a source of a workforce. And many companies are turning here to do just that. Many of the workers come from less-developed countries in the Indian sub-continent, and Asia, where a dollar goes a lot further than it does in more developed, Western countries. That means an employer can take on multiple casual workers for less than a full-timer, without the need to pay for holidays, sickness, pensions, or any of the other on-costs of employment. Employing people from around the globe has never been easier. Neither has releasing them from work.

This will increase feelings of both empowerment and insecurity amongst global workforces. But which will your colleagues experience? And what impact will that have on the capacity of your business? How many jobs can be outsourced in this manner, and how many might be better completed in-house by a permanent member of staff?

Zero-hour contracts are another example of a new working pattern that has delivered benefits to some employees and organisations, but headache and heartache to others.

In response to these shifting trends, pioneering organisations are learning, adapting, and creating new forms of employment that offer both flexibility and security. There are plenty of examples of people choosing how they want to work depending on their life stage and circumstances and, for example, contracting to work three months per year so they can also meet their other life priorities. This provides a socially responsible approach to the gig economy. Organisations that can learn to understand, respond and leverage changing working relationships for the benefit of *both* parties can benefit enormously.

What is lost to companies is the learning and adaptation of tasks to their individual setting. If *ad hoc* gig working is adopted, there is a constant need to train in 'our way of doing it'. The economy of paying someone new to work remotely on a job-by-job basis may be offset by the time it takes to integrate them into the company culture and methods every time. Learning time equals money in training time.

Looking at these brief examples (and there are many, many others) it becomes clear how learning and development – be it on organisational or personal levels – has a vital role to play in enabling businesses to grow as they build sustainable cultures, infrastructure, and support mechanisms. And it is only through learning that firms will be able to develop a culture that encourages the things that will become key differentiators in 4IR; namely joined-up thinking, creativity, and collaboration.

THE CURRENT STATE OF LEARNING & DEVELOPMENT

It is important to examine where learning is currently positioned and how it is perceived within industry. First, let us revisit our definition of OL&D – the mantra that should drive learning in the Fourth Industrial Revolution. We consider it to be:

> *The process by which an organisation improves itself over time through gaining real-time experience, creating and transferring knowledge, improving skills and enabling behaviour change. This is a planned and systematic approach that enables sustained organisation performance through the involvement of its people.*

By following this credo, we can begin to design and deliver learning strategies that will maximise people performance, solve the business problems, add customer value, and create an organisational culture that ensures a business's success.

A useful metaphor to describe the delivery of learning in the world of 4IR is one of manoeuvring a yacht. At sea you need to be constantly monitoring, assessing and adapting to changes in the surrounding elements, whilst heading towards a particular destination. Whether it is a sudden squall, mountainous waves, or dead calm (or that enormous shadow swimming just beneath the surface) those elements will keep throwing new and unexpected challenges your way. It is your job to anticipate those as best you can but keep working to ensure you remain resolutely on course for your goal.

To stretch the metaphor, we often hear that 'we are all in the same boat'. No, we aren't. We might be on the same waves some of the time, but we are certainly not in the same boat. Individual organisations and sectors are in different boats, going at different speeds, and in different directions.

The unfortunate truth is that within the vast flotilla of yachts represented by learning practitioners and proponents, there are a large number not seaworthy. Some vessels are holed below the waterline, others in need of urgent repair, and yet more are trying to work out how the radar works and what on earth that big rock-like thing is just ahead. There are some however, who have set a course and are using the conditions to their advantage.

The overriding belief of the learning function is that it has been until recent times a transactional role, when it should be transformational as it develops people – and hence organisations – for the future. However, there is a problem when it comes to measurement of L&D activities and gaining valuable insights about the impact of learning. We'll talk a lot about the importance of analytical capabilities and using an evidence base (including the kinds of insights that will help you drive success) as we go on. We can't say it enough: data and AI are crucial and L&D professionals are playing catch up. But for now, know that if you are not knee-deep in data, you are not alone. In recent research:

- only 16% of L&D departments reported having a dedicated data analyst
- only 19% of learning professionals use analytics to improve their offering[19]
- only 10% reported using performance data to measure the impact of their programs.[20]

All of which highlights a worrying lack of understanding and evidence building in the profession at a time when customer, employee and learner data should form a core element of learning activity. If the profession is to step up and be a game-changer in 4IR it has to be able to demonstrate its contribution to business outcomes; it has to prove its importance to the company and its customers.

Other sobering statistics that should prompt any conscientious practitioner to consider changing what they do and how they do it:

- The number one metric used by CEOs to evaluate L&D effectiveness is business impact and second is return on investment. [21]
- Only about one in three millennials and Gen Z staff believe that they have 'all the skills and knowledge they'll need' for a world being shaped by Industry 4.0.[22] This figure is one in five when considering all workers.[23]

The LinkedIn Workplace Learning Report 2023 shows only 26% of the workforce say their organisation challenged them to learn a new skill. When we put these statistics to several HR and Learning leaders, there was very little surprise. In fact, Ingo Perizonius, People Development Director at EDF Energy says, 'We as learning professionals have failed as experts in the learning industry, let's become serious about data and changing the perception and reality of learning.' This belief is shared by many other senior learning professionals including Cathy Strachan MBE who asks 'How have we let ourselves get in this position? We have to be courageous.'

Contrast that with this statement from Leena Nair, Global CEO of Chanel, a pioneer in the learning space. She was the first female, first Asian, and youngest ever, Chief Human Resource Officer at Unilever. Her thoughts on 4IR, technology, and data are clear, as are the methods needed to get buy-in from the business:

> *Making smarter use of technology requires a solid understanding of people data... We have to use data to talk tangibly about the impact of technology. No one will give you free money to play with*

> *if there is no business case... For example, the HR team at Unilever is able to quantify that for every $1 invested in health and wellbeing initiatives, they get a return of $2.50. That's the sort of information that makes the board pay attention.*[24]

There are challenges, but the current condition of organisational learning and development also presents the opportunity of a lifetime. There is no better time to:

- play a key role in the successful transformation of your business
- link people and their performance to technology
- calculate that elusive ROI that informs business decisions.

There is so much upside to this! So much opportunity for OL&D to become a symbol of great change, to question the status quo and change things for the better. In uncertain times, the nature of risk changes. It is the risk of *not* doing something that may well be greater. Inertia is the enemy. As Rahm Emanuel said, 'You never want a serious crisis go to waste... [it is an] opportunity to do things that you could not do before.'[25] 4IR does not need to be seen as a crisis, but it will be a time of uncertainty and change that will demand the kind of behaviour that Rahm advocates. We must learn to adapt, to take our chances when they come, and to thrive.

Change – and the accompanying risk – is *good.* Change can be made. It *should* be made. Let us grasp that change and make this new era a time to redefine the role, impact and reputation of the learning and development function.

TO INFINITY AND BEYOND

Peter Cheese, CEO at CIPD, told me:

> *Learning is entering the perfect storm, a once-in-a-lifetime opportunity to make a meaningful difference to the world of work.*

The truth is, the political, economic, social, and technological forces that shape our daily lives are aligning in favour of OL&D. It is a great time to be in the business of learning. It is time to reinvent ourselves as drivers of innovation and productivity, of customer experience, of employability, and of corporate performance – even corporate relevance.

No longer will we deliver learning just for the sake of education, knowledge, or compliance. Now, we will solve business problems, add customer value, improve performance, and drive the bottom line. We will face up to rapidly changing technology and workplaces and use our understanding of them to help shape and design businesses, by aligning organisational goals with the practical and personalised skills needs of individuals. And we will deliver this in real time.

We say it again: this is not a tech agenda – it is a people agenda. This era of rapid technological evolution and integration will not be about 'tech first', it will be about 'people first', because that's where the strategic advantage lies. Lots of businesses have (and will no doubt continue) investing in tech, be it for learning or anything else, without finding the business impact that leadership is looking for. This approach fails, as we have said already, because their starting point is the latest tech, when it should be addressing a business problem, improving customer value, or some other core performance metric.

You can neatly sidestep this trap by designing your learning around sales pipelines, new innovations, or whatever matters to your business. You can future-proof your activities by asking what new skills are required going forward to deliver those products or services. In doing so, you begin that process of shaping organisational design based on the skills for the future, in turn linking development to performance.

If it sounds like a big job, it is. But you won't be the first to try it. Not by a long shot.

CHANGING THE LEARNING INDUSTRY

There are plenty of examples of energetic and proactive businesses that are working to redefine the role of learning in organisations. We have come across pockets of true inspiration on our travels; organisations that are thriving in spite (or perhaps because) of current challenges.

Their approach to OL&D is different and we have much to learn from them. The fact these businesses (which we will look at in depth later on) may not be in your industry or sector is immaterial. They are the innovators that have spent the time, money and energy on doing things differently. They have pioneered new models – and seen their fair share of failure along the way. You can learn from them and future-proof your organisation, comparing their strategies and priorities with your own as you go. The new perspective they offer you can become a springboard to the design and implementation of valuable behavioural and cultural change throughout your business.

The inexorable drive towards digital – and increased remote working – offers a powerful example of such progressive and business-orientated activities in action. Many learning and development professionals we have spoken to are focused on supporting employee wellbeing and resilience in this new paradigm, as a way of maintaining mental health levels, while also boosting productivity. Elsewhere, they are facilitating the dramatic increase in flexible working by upskilling leaders to manage teams remotely, helping them devolve decision-making to their people, and shifting focus to measuring performance based on the outcomes of this new behaviour.

The real pioneers are taking the opportunity to focus on the future in a far broader sense. We have seen, first-hand, learning professionals creating opportunities for people across their companies to collaborate and have the conversations needed to solve the problems the business faces. They are coaching and giving leaders insights around the human needs of employees during transformational change. We have seen them facilitating these conversations while, at the same time, joining up the learning points in terms of leadership, culture, and their organisation's purpose.

We have seen learning professionals using the context of sudden change to make the case for, and develop, their business' capacity to shape future-focused skills; such as critical thinking, problem solving and decision-making at all levels. In one case a learning leader asked how their firm could use the situation to accelerate digital capabilities and what support they could offer for that.

This engagement spilled into other areas, such as looking at:

- improving the resilience of supply chains
- how they might collaborate with non-competing organisations to close skills gaps
- giving insights on employee engagement and wellbeing through big data, using the voice of the employee (and even customers) to aid decision making.

Whilst in these forums they were also ensuring customer and people strategies were aligned to the company's purpose and values. As such, they were seeing each conversation as a chance to develop the organisational culture, supporting leaders to reflect, learn and embed a new style of leadership.

There were numerous examples of these pioneers consciously creating opportunities for people to connect and collaborate, to harness the collective intelligence and creativity of their people to solve challenges, look for trends, and change skill levels and behaviours – all in the flow of people's daily work.

We've seen them uniting colleagues as an inclusive community with a common purpose – a community where people felt they belonged, no matter the storms raging around them. We've seen OL&D acting as a guide – and even leading an organisation's strategy on occasion. They used people analytics to give insights that would allow colleagues to understand the world they are working in, enabling them to make better decisions, and mould the workplace to make it more effective. To make that work, they were helping to tell the story of what was going on, as well as helping explain where the organisation was going. As such, learning professionals were helping create a vision that sustained the business's narrative and helped drive the essence of 'who are we, where have we come from, where are we going, and why'.

In these pioneering organisations every approach was different and was facilitated within a wider framework of each company's culture, vision, purpose, values and goals. But all these pioneers shared the courage to have difficult conversations with senior leaders to show how the commercial indicators connected to human indicators, and hence demonstrate how their work made sense in a commercial context.

In these firms we do *not* see learning being driven solely by a traditional L&D or HR service model. We see partnership. We see learning being championed by almost anyone in the business – from the Head of Operations, Engineering or Customer Experience, to the recently-promoted team leader or CEO – all within a dynamic learning infrastructure put in place by learning experts.

We cite these examples of proactive and productive change to show it can be done. But they also reveal the scale of the challenge for many – to maintain their strategic focus and influence the direction of their business.

WE NEED TO BE IN THE FLOW

One of our key tactics in how we deliver learning must be personalisation. When Josh Bersin looked into corporate learning back in 2015, he found that among the 700+ organisations studied, the average employee only had 24 minutes a week for 'formal learning'.[26] We probably have even less now. He focused on design thinking and agile practices to distil what he called 'high impact' and 'highly relevant' adaptive learning practices. He went on to describe the move to micro learning, which embraced emerging learning and development technology as 'learning in the flow of work' – learning opportunities delivered in bite-sized formats that flow seamlessly into the daily work routine.[27]

It feels like the rest of the world has now caught up (and we will take a close look shortly at one firm that has transformed learning using a similar approach). The comparison often made with Netflix is apt: it knows where you left off, what you like to engage with and what you don't. You can watch something on that platform for a few minutes or you can binge watch for hours.

Transferred into a work context, this equates to understanding what, how and when an individual prefers their learning content. They may want to engage via videos, TED Talks, articles, graphics, games, Google searches or any mixture of these. It means knowing whether they like learning in the mornings or the evening; whether they actively search for it or are best prompted. Ultimately it means optimising your use of people's time so learning becomes part of the flow of their work and productivity is not interrupted. People learn – and then apply that learning – while working, rather than being taken off the job to do it.

This approach is an easy idea to sell to business leaders, as the number one barrier given to learning is usually time.

Sophisticated learning systems are able to gauge how people learn best. As we collect more data and gain more insights, we will be able to understand our colleagues' profiles, interests, and development needs, and align those with future business needs. This will give us an ever-clearer picture of what people want to learn, how they want to learn, and when they need to learn. From this we will be able to ingrain a habit and culture of everyday learning.

As we go into more detail on this through the book, we will see that this principle of learning at the point of need continues to evolve.

Human beings learn and remember through emotionally significant events and experiences. We also delete things that are not important or significant to us personally. Therefore, we need to ensure we must tap into people's emotions, what is important to them and what they are concerned about, if we are going to connect and support people to engage, learn and change a capability or behaviour.

We are not just talking about filling gaps in knowledge quickly and effectively anymore. Pioneers are looking at ways to encourage 'connected thinking': empowering employees to join up dots and see patterns that they would never have seen before, in turn enabling them to drive innovation and productivity as never before.

These learning pioneers are providing frameworks that ensure when decisions are made or being made, they can be analysed in the context of the key skills the company needs to thrive in 4IR. Better still, others are making sure they're in the room at the time so opportunities to understand, learn and contextualise decisions in accordance with the firm's long-term skills needs aren't missed. This is a style of adaptive learning called 'real-time learning' and we'll look at what it means in depth below.

All that said, don't put all your eggs in the 'flow' or 'real-time' learning baskets just yet. We must remember that deeper learning (the kind that can deliver lasting changes in habit and behaviour) still requires the time and effort to help people step back, reflect, unpick their learning needs, and create a plan with support. For behavioural change we often need experiences that are outside our normal daily routine, support to understand them, and ongoing support to embed these changes. It is often this kind of change that will facilitate the development of skills crucial to the 4IR era: critical thinking, problem solving, and decision-making, as well as the development of new styles of leadership.

Ultimately, this all comes back to a relentless focus on your audience and their needs. As such, we would recommend that when you come to designing your systems, processes and output you could do worse than considering a variation on design thinking (which we mentioned above), a human-centred process for creative problem solving. It encourages organisations to focus on the people that the solution is made for. It combines creative and critical thinking that allows ideas to be organised, decisions to be made, solutions to be found, and knowledge to be gained. This approach could greatly aid your efforts to deliver learning that integrates into the flow of their colleagues' work.

Let us look at how one company completely changed the nature of its L&D team to meet this challenge.

CASE STUDY: THE TRANSFORMATION OF SANTANDER BANK'S L&D

Santander is a great example of a company that is adopting many of the lessons set out in this book. The bank has transformed in its L&D capability, putting itself at the forefront of the modern profession. We'll come back to the bank on a few occasions to highlight different ways they went about achieving this, but one of the most important changes that Robert Ashcroft, Head of Capability (the department formerly known as Learning & Development) made was restructuring and reprioritising how his team works:

> *I didn't – and still don't – want to eradicate the importance of academic study and the academic approach to learning, but when I looked at*

> *what we were doing back in 2018 I felt corporate L&D had lost its way. It had become the oracle – the purveyor of all knowledge. Our approach was: I'll bring 15 people in, I'll stand at the front and I'll talk at you, we'll do some role-plays, and so on. We had got into this monotony of 60-odd training rooms, 60-odd trainers – all very routine.*

When Robert looked at the world around him, he saw YouTube, social media, and other mechanisms creating a hyper-connected environment in which people were constantly learning from one another. He realised that this new paradigm did not chime with traditional learning, which he believes is 'almost like parent to child, reminiscent of school'. It was time for change.

WHAT SANTANDER DID

Robert's strategy put a new focus on delivering development experiences that fostered self-sufficiency and were integrated into colleagues' daily work.

The Capability team delivered a learning strategy that was defined by three stages: experience, reflection, and action.

If Robert's team were to succeed in making what was, at the time, a radical change to how L&D did business, they would need to be able to design learning products that facilitated this approach.

The starting point is always to know what people care about. Therefore, the learning opportunity needs to be an experience that is designed to be something significant to the individuals and the organisation. We learn from our own experiences, through trial and error and successes; also through observing the experiences of others or hearing the stories about other people's experiences. Individuals often learn better in teams: if you work and learn together at the same time you create a culture of learning; a significant collective experience.

To achieve this, the team adopted a process of product development akin to industrial design, mixing design learning with agile and lean theory. Getting this right meant changing how the department operated. Learning consultants were renamed Product Owners and individuals were handed responsibility for the design and delivery of the different learning products. As such, each owner became responsible for the entire lifecycle of his or her product.

> *We now operate as a collective of independent product owners who work together and share our learnings as we go,' says Robert. 'Each product owner recognises that they are building a product or a service that needs to be consumed and they are the owner of it – not some senior management or the learning department; them. They know that if they own it, it's up to them to care about it and regularly check that it's doing what it's supposed to do – and, if it's not, do something about it.*

The quality bar for these products is very high we will look later at just how high when we address modern expectations of L&D. Robert's product owners achieved that by engaging deeply with those who would be using them.

> *Your biggest critic isn't a stakeholder or a senior staff member who has commissioned a piece of work,' Robert says. 'It's the people that you're actually getting to engage in your product who you take through the construct, the prototype, the minimum viable proposition (MVP). Then you've got to take the first product out to them to check it still does what they think it's going to do. That level of scrutiny is relentless. It puts the fear into most of my product owners because people share what they think.*

It may seem like there's a lot to take in here, but Robert believes it is the core principle that learning cannot and should not be divorced from the modern, hyper-connected world that matters most. If you can build around that, you will see great improvements in how learning is delivered.

> *Development is often so micro and incremental – it doesn't need to be this big paradigm shift in ability,' he says. 'It's about real-time learning and seizing those opportunities when they're available; it's about being consciously aware of what's happened, taking stock, thinking about it, and making decisions based on what you've learnt. Our job is to facilitate that.*

The fundamental shift in how Santander's Capability Department does business is clear in how it recruits:

> *We recruit on values: do you care, do you have a strong sense of accountability, do you have a passion for continuous improvement, do you actively embrace change and agility?' says Robert. 'We don't recruit for learning professionals any more, we recruit for people who want to do those things as part of their job – they just so happen to do those things as part of a learning team.*

Santander's experience offers insight into the kind of approach that we believe lie at the heart of learning and development functions that will be fit for the world of 4IR. But before you get into designing an integrated learning system, there are some bigger questions to address. Perhaps the biggest – and most daunting – question of all being: 'where on earth to start?' Happily, we have the answer.

A NEW FORMULA FOR YOUR SUCCESS

THE 'WHAT'

The forward-looking organisations we have described are as varied as they are unique. They range from global logistics businesses to telecommunications giants, from department stores, to financial services companies, and entire health systems. But as we have studied them, we have discovered they all demonstrate an approach to learning that comprises five common elements. We have taken these common elements and distilled them into the acronym 'CAPEX', a formula designed to turn learning into an asset that any business would be foolish to ignore. CAPEX stands for:

Culture
Adaptability
Purpose
Expectations
X-Factor

In the next section, we will examine each of these elements and why they are important to organisations that want to thrive:

- In **Culture**, we look at organisations using their learning functions to create positive, high-performance, high-trust cultures, and what the benefits of this approach are.
- In **Adaptability** we explore the ever-greater need for organisations, teams, and individuals to be flexible, agile, responsive, resilient… and to keep things simple.
- **Purpose** lies at the heart of CAPEX, and here we will look at how this concept helps generate engagement, focus and commitment, and drives commercial success.
- In **Expectations** we examine how expectations (and the experiences) that people have of organisations are changing, and the

opportunities this gives those responsible for learning to reinvent themselves and what they deliver.

- In **X-Factor**, we explore how you can harness the creativity, collaboration and innovation that naturally arise from harnessing the elements above to help your business evolve and thrive.

We will put each part of the CAPEX formula in the context of the crucial role learning should play in ensuring each of these elements is embedded in the DNA of the organisation – and how every individual employee can play their part in ensuring that learning is used effectively.

THE 'HOW'

The CAPEX formula will give you an in-depth understanding of what you need to thrive in the new world of learning and development. We will then move onto looking at how you can bring that theory to life. We will examine how you can reshape your strategies and tactics to embed the new learning paradigm we have discussed. We will also look at how you can hit the ground running, gain support for your new strategy, and embed it in your organisation.

For ease, we will explore CAPEX in a linear sequence (from C to X). But it is helpful to picture the model above as an inter-linked process rather than a straight line. The five CAPEX elements are mutually supportive and mutually dependent. They do not operate in a vacuum. The ideal scenario is to eventually have all five CAPEX elements woven into the day-to-day life of the business. Therefore, we stress that for organisations wishing to adapt these elements for themselves, *there is no right or wrong place to start.*

Each organisation will have their own needs and requirements. For example, one business may see a pressing need to work on its Purpose – in which case, that element will be the primary focus. Meanwhile, another might realise that Adaptability is key to beginning their transition, so they should start there.

Once the work on one element has begun, it will become apparent which of the other four elements needs to be introduced and worked on next. Thanks to the way the different elements of CAPEX naturally support one another, they begin to have a compounding effect as new elements are introduced. The result will be far greater than the sum of its individual parts.

Current and emerging technologies will be your companion on this journey (and if they're not, then you're missing out on a crucial piece of the future of work jigsaw). If you aren't already getting stuck in, you and your organisation will soon be getting to grips with various platforms, from traditional learning management systems (LMS), to modern learning experience platforms (LXP) and learning apps, which allow you to deliver learning in the flow of your colleagues' day-to-day work.

At risk of getting carried away, it may not be long before you're talking in terms of augmented reality, perhaps with virtual coaches guiding your colleagues through technical aspect of their role as they perform it, offering 'just in time' performance support. And, while we are here, why shouldn't you take advantage of knowledge engines that could be tracking knowledge inside and outside your organisation, before offering integrated micro-courses that learn from those taking them and adapt to keep training relevant, fresh and interesting? Are trainees better with a more traditional form of training? Fine. Would they respond better to a gamified version of the same information? Sure thing. How about a virtual reality workplace, where learners and avatars interact? Oh, go on then.

The technological route you choose to take will be determined by your needs and, of course, your budget. But even the most basic tech-based training programmes will put the kind of power in your hands that would leave the jaws of previous generations of L&D professionals on the floor.

THE 'WHY'

Wherever you decide to start with CAPEX and whatever tech you use, it is crucial that you construct your approach so that you can use data and analytics to show why you're making the choice you are, and the results those choices are bringing in. We've already touched on how the future success of learning will rely on the ability to work towards specific business outcomes, using data to show demonstrable value from your activities. And you'll hear us say time and again that learning has been let down in the past because its activities, while intuitively valuable, could not be proved empirically. As Vidya Krishnan, Chief Learning Officer and Global Head of Learning and Development at Ericsson, says:

> *Learning is oxygen – invisible but necessary to survive. Analytics will make it visible.*[28]

A decade after big data became a buzzword, most organisations are fighting to build insight-driven cultures, based on the reams of data they generate. No one should make decisions based on a mere hunch or gut feeling any more. Learning is no exception. And the insight is there for the taking.

Most people start with performance management data and analytics in their bid to drive business value. There are lots more areas where data could afford you the opportunity to demonstrate the business value, ROI and learning, as well as align with, and help influence, business strategy, goals and success. Let us look at some examples of that in action and some strategic questions:

- Analysing the voice of the employee and customer provides insight on the needs, wishes and sentiment of employees and customers alike, this can be done in the moment in many cases. How can these insights be fed into conversations, decisions and learning programmes that facilitate changes in behaviours, productivity and performance?

- Where are the reported skills shortages in your organisation? Can you match skillsets – gleaned from learning and HR data – with project or role opportunities (and, consequently, encourage greater mobility within the organisation and more agile responses)? Moreover, can you predict what experiences people will want or what career they desire?
- Is there an optimal time in a role? How long do you need colleagues to be in situ before they are great at it? How can you speed that process up using learning? And how can you encourage people to stay in that role until at least that time?
- Is there a link between learning hours and attrition? For example, are leavers from the organisation spending less time learning?
- Does increasing or decreasing (certain types of) learning impact on staff retention?
- Can you connect patterns of collaboration and changes in relationship connections with longevity, or with people leaving the organisation? There is often a link between people's reduction in relationship contact and activity and exiting the organisation a short time later. This happens because relationships connect people to the culture and the organisation, and if these connections drop off then the individual could be disconnecting. If activity is reducing, it is an opportunity to have a conversation with the individual with a view to increasing retention. This data can also be used to track new starters and see how they develop their networks and how inclusive the business is.
- Does your data show a link between investing in people's wellbeing and the reduction in stress, absence and sickness?
- Can the analysis of feedback from people leaving your organisation who you want to keep, provide valuable information that can help improve future retention, optimise the employee experience, and determine ways to drive significant cultural change within an organisation?

- Is there a connection between net promoter scores (NPS) and the amount of learning an individual undertakes?
- Is there a link between how quickly a customer answers a communication from you with the depth of relationship and the sales growth and customer retention?
- Inclusion is all about finding out whether your employees feel they belong. Do your employees feel engaged with your business? If not, why not? What impact is this having on productivity? Inclusion is often closely related to diversity. Perhaps your data shows that diverse teams in your business deliver greater performance or innovation? How can you spread such knowledge?
- Figures on performance in, for example, gender equity and equality, could also be the difference between a major investor deciding to put their money into your firm, or not. Again, what do you need to do to improve understanding and acceptance of diversity?
- *What does analysis of skills levels in areas critical for future growth show?* And how do these metrics stand up against competitors across the industry? How does this comparison change over time?
- Who in the organisation is encouraging others to learn and develop, and how can we recognise these leaders? People like this can be crucial in creating a culture of learning.

Using examples like this, you can take all that unstructured data and interpret it in the context of your CAPEX priorities. This will enable you to identify themes and patterns that can shape the way your organisation does business.

You will now have evidence to back up what your gut instinct (but not necessarily everyone else) knew to be true in the past: that learning is at the heart of all great organisations. The opportunity to learn and grow is what attracts the best people, enables the most effective and innovative decision-making, and drives long-term business value. Data – and the ability to interpret it – will turn you into the L&D equivalent of a top sportsperson. Yes, you will know where the ball is now, but you will also be able to anticipate where it will be in two or three phases time.

At some point in this process, you will find yourself a fully-fledged, insight driven business partner, providing analysis that drives decision-making, solves business problems, and future-proofs your organisation.

THE CAPEX FORMULA

So, the five pillars that will drive successful organisational learning in the Fourth Industrial Revolution are:

Culture
Adaptability
Purpose
Expectations
X-Factor

We've looked in some depth at the status quo and we've looked at a vision of where learning go could and what the profession could achieve. But if we were to sum up everything, we would say simply this:

> *If you take the pillars of CAPEX, plug them into your organisational goals using solid data analytics for support, then the 4IR world will be your oyster.*

CAPEX – 'C' IS FOR CULTURE

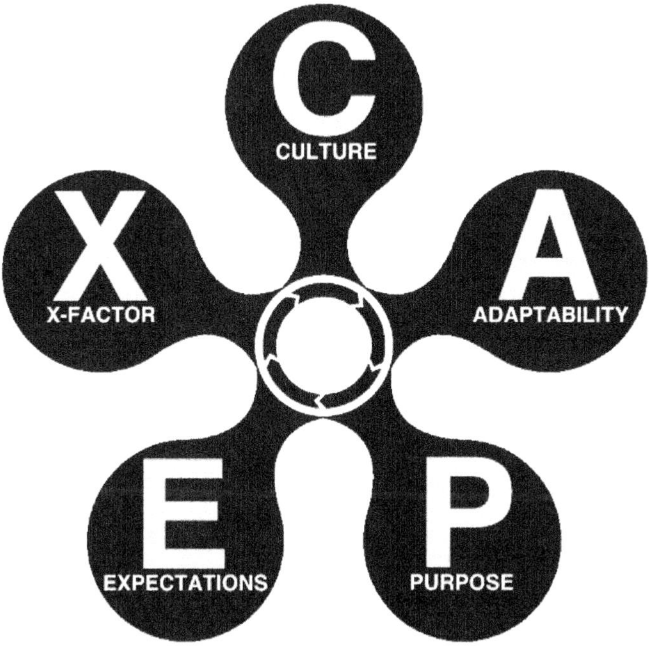

If there was a single message or impression we would want you to take away from this section it would be this: organisational culture matters more than it ever has before. Ever. In human history.

Of course, people and culture have always been bound together, whether we are talking about organisational cultures or our wider societal cultures. In both instances, people influence and impact culture, and culture influences and impacts people. It is a constantly evolving, dynamic relationship.

Culture is a way of life, and a way of work. It is the way we treat each other, it is our behaviour in different circumstances, it is the way we solve problems, create and innovate, and the way we make decisions. It is critical to social, political, and economic success at every level; from individual to team, organisation and wider society. In the context of our discussion, it is the organisation's personality. It provides context for everything the business does and it drives the environment everyone exists in. As such, culture is a key determinant of whether individuals will sink or swim, or whether the business will flounder or flourish. For all these reasons, it is said that 'culture eats brand strategy for lunch'.

Global logistics firm FedEx Express is a great example of how important a positive culture is in 4IR. Their approach to culture building has helped them win numerous awards, including places on Fortune's 'World's Most Admired Companies', '100 Best Companies to Work For', and 'Best Big Companies to Work For' lists. It has made them one of the most reputable and successful companies in the world.

One of the four core pillars upon which FedEx Express culture is built is learning. The importance of the company's culture to everything they do is designed to be embedded throughout the firm's processes and systems. Employees have many opportunities to hit cultural touch points that remind them of the values the firm holds dear. All managers are expected to embed the company culture and lead continuous learning in their teams.

When asked what this means in the context of building a positive, resilient culture, Trevor Hoyle, Senior Vice President for FedEx Express Operations in Europe, said:

> *As an operational senior manager, I see leading the strategy on learning as a key part of my role with the support and expertise of my specialist learning colleagues. The strategic importance of*

learning now and in the future is shown in it being one of our four pillars and central to our goals of:

- *creating a great place to work*
- *facilitating innovation*
- *enabling people to take smart risks*
- *enabling quick and agile decision-making.*

Hundreds of cultural ambassadors exist to spread the word globally. This way, the company's culture remains a living, breathing entity that drives FedEx Express forward and creates a virtuous circle where the firm connects learning to its culture, its culture to its people, its people to the customer experience, and customer experience back to the brand.

But creating the right culture for a thriving business is no easy task. It requires large amounts of listening, self-reflection, honesty, clear communication, and authentic leadership. But it is perfectly possible and the ROI – which we will refer to relentlessly – is there for all to see when it is done right. Those organisations that are doing it right are using Organisational Learning & Development (OL&D) to create positive, inclusive, healthy, high-trust, high-performance cultures – cultures in which people and business can learn, adapt and grow, no matter the circumstances.

In the Fourth Industrial Revolution (4IR), culture in forward-thinking companies is not something that is imposed on people, as was prevalent in the command and control hierarchies that characterised earlier industrial revolutions. Now culture is led by people. It is for people.

This new dynamic is having far-reaching consequences. For example, did you notice something different about how many governments around the world responded to both the pandemic and the Russian military invasion of Ukraine? With surprising consistency, it was citizens who were put first, not institutions or vested interests. Governments showed themselves willing to put health and lives before finance. This gave a sense that vested interests and elites could not sway decisions in a way they might once have done. We would argue this was an approach that was pioneered in the private sector, which is always quicker to respond to societal shifts than its public counterpart, out of sheer necessity. But the way governments behaved also reinforced a powerful cultural message: our cultures are becoming more caring, more human-centric entities.

There is an irony in the fact that, as technology continues its relentless march, we are seeing a cultural shift that takes us closer to a 'human-led' model, rather than further away. This model values individuals and it demands that they are given identity, purpose, recognition and a host of other needs. If you think your organisation is immune from this, you are badly mistaken. This is the over-arching culture that will come to characterise 4IR. Creating a workplace culture fit for the new world of work.

The 4IR-ready, learning professional sees him or herself as the guardian of the culture. To achieve this, you will need to be coaching, developing and facilitating the culture in every conversation, meeting you have or decision you make. Your entire approach will need aligning with driving culture.

In practical terms, this means focusing on developing learning as a continuous behaviour that enables individuals and teams to develop and drive a high-performance culture that is aligned with the personality of the firm.

The nuances of each personality will be different from firm to firm, but there are key cultural trends that are common to firms thriving in 4IR and which you can use at the foundations of your approach to facilitating a high-performance culture. These trends are:

- Employee wellbeing and a caring workplace
- Encouraging positivity and happiness
- Enabling a high-trust environment.

Let us explore each in turn.

EMPLOYEE WELLBEING AND A CARING WORKPLACE

Employee wellbeing is becoming an ever-more important aspect of organisational culture, which is a positive thing. However, the driver for this is not pure altruism; it has grown out of rapid changes in the way we live and work. While our bodies might not be being challenged in the way workers might have found in previous industrial revolutions (except perhaps through lack of use due to our often-sedentary lifestyles), our minds are under tremendous pressure. This includes through that strange and counterintuitive consequence of ever-greater connectivity: we feel more alone than ever before.

For quite some time our work practices have shown symptoms of malaise when it comes to employee wellbeing and care. High on the list of reasons for this is our 'always on' culture, which has been driven by advances in technology and our inability to balance greater speed and connectivity with the need to step back and switch off.

People's inability to disconnect from work – the perceived need to always be contactable – can cause immense stress and anxiety in terms of work expectations, and has a measurable impact on turnover. To that we can add other traits like perfectionism, fear of failure, and job insecurity. As you can imagine, the impact on wellbeing – and therefore on productivity – is far from ideal.

Hybrid working allows people to work from home, saving two or three hours of their day commuting. For some people this makes life easier, but many do not take the opportunity to shorten their working hours, they just start earlier and finish later. As the boundaries between home and work became even more blurred, routine and balance can be lost, and the risk of burnout increased. These warning signs are important lessons for the future. If we let this mission creep continue then the promise of 4IR benefits, such as three- or four-hour working days (as tech takes up the slack) will never be realised. The hours will simply be filled by other tasks and our wellbeing, and that of our colleagues will continue to be strained.

Research conducted by Opinion Matters on behalf of GFI Software confirms how badly the lines between work and home life have become blurred:

- Over four in five of us check our work emails on weekends, while more than half do so past 11 p.m.
- Almost 60% deal with their work email while on holiday.
- As many as 64% of us check their work email at least daily during out-of-office hours.
- A full 12% of us check their email in real time outside working hours, never truly switching off.[29]

In the UK, the CIPD, which represents companies employing almost five million people, found that technology prevents 87% of us from switching off out of work hours, often leaving them stressed, anxious, or fearful.[30] In a similar vein, the '2020 World Happiness Report' revealed that general 'worry' has increased by 8–10% in the last nine years.[31]

We risk turning this trend into a vicious circle since, under these conditions, people's 'threat response' kicks in, and they become more self-focused and insular, and are less likely to seek support. They feel increasingly trapped in what they are doing; and that's something you must combat through your programs, because people need to feel freedom and not fear if they are going to perform at their best.

This can encourage presenteeism – the act of showing up to work sick, injured, overly fatigued or otherwise not operating at normal levels of productivity. Research shows that presenteeism due to illness, depression or other ailments is a common but often unaddressed issue that can be costly.

There is also the phenomenon of 'leaveism' to be considered. This term, first coined in 2014 by Dr Ian Hesketh and Cary L. Cooper, of the University of Manchester, refers to employees using holiday and other time-off allocations instead of sick leave. Moreover, it includes employees finishing their work at home or using holiday time to catch up on uncompleted tasks.[32, 33]

To combat this, many forward-thinking organisations are offering unlimited paid time off; if performance is delivered, and the business is not disrupted. For some employees this works well, for others the uncertainty leads to stress, anxiety and taking less time off rather than more.

The American Institute of Stress reported that a staggering 80% of staff experience regular stress at work.[34] Per Eastern Kentucky University, this costs US employers more than $300bn a year.[35] In the book *Dying for a Paycheck,* Stanford business professor Jeffrey Pfeffer lays out the terrible consequences: workplace stress in the United States is the fifth-highest cause of death.[36]

THE IMPORTANCE OF CARING

To avoid further stressing an already vulnerable workforce, now, more than ever, we need to recognise and address the impact 4IR is having on wellbeing, and work to shift business cultures from 'threat' to 'thrive'. Helping people to learn the skills to empower them to work better, as well as giving them the tools to build positive, resilient mindsets to cope with life's challenges and adapt to adversity. This approach must be at the heart of your culture-building efforts.

We can turn again to FedEx Express to look at a practical and highly successful application of wellbeing. Just as learning is a core cultural pillar for the firm, so is caring. The firm puts great emphasis on employees doing the right thing, caring about the wellbeing of their colleagues and having respect for each other. This does not just mean being nice all the time. Emma Wright VP HR at FedEx Express in Memphis makes clear, for example, that the firm expects colleagues to be able to have courageous conversations with one another when required, but this must be done with the right intentions and care enough to deliver the message in the right way.

So, at first sight, you might think a 24-hour, global operation like FedEx Express is a prime candidate for falling into the many traps that exist in a 4IR world of relentless speed and constant connectivity. But instead of hearing a litany of complaints from disgruntled, burnt-out staff, you are more likely to hear applause as FedEx Express is once again ranked as one of the most attractive places to work. A culture built on learning and caring is a crucial reason for that.

The key aspect to all this remains the realisation that the most powerful lever you have for success – your people – are not machines. They will require nurturing and protection in 4IR. Getting this right will boost engagement, productivity, innovation and a host of other benefits that will directly drive business success.

As sensible as this all might seem, embedding employee wellbeing can be difficult. Organisational cultures are often deeply ingrained and the result of an approach to work that may have served firms well in the past, but which is no longer relevant. You might find the notion of addressing wellbeing is positively alien to some senior leadership. This, incidentally, is where your data on the impact of wellbeing, or lack thereof, will prove vital.

The way people approach employee wellbeing has changed radically over the decades. In the 1990s and early 2000s many leaders thought mental toughness was the key to success and creating a thriving workplace culture. This notion developed into a mantra of 'soak up the pressure and be tenacious', before experts began to focus on resilience and the ability to learn and adapt so you can bounce back from setbacks. More recent developments in the field reflect an increasing need to look at resilience in terms of the whole person: their physical, mental, emotional, financial, social and relationships resilience.

A joint accountability has emerged as a mark of human-led cultures; where individuals need to look out for both themselves and their colleagues, under the umbrella of an organisation that is looking after the wellbeing and resilience of all its people. In each of these categories you have a crucial role to play in nurturing an environment where workplace experiences – both good and bad – can be highlighted and reflected upon in the moment; new knowledge acquired; and appropriate ownership, decisions and behavioural changes implemented.

Those businesses leading the way are supporting employees in numerous different ways, as suit their circumstances. These support activities include learning to find a better work-life balance; financial coaching, training members of the team to be mental health coaches and counsellors (or providing specialist professionals); developing the skills to manage your mood and mindset, or offering yoga and mindfulness sessions. The list of initiatives is growing all the time.

As ever, there is plenty of tech on offer you help you deliver on your wellbeing agenda. Companies can buy corporate licenses for their employees to use programs that help them meditate, stay fit, and maintain a healthy diet, all while giving them 24/7 access to therapy and resources. The market is overflowing with apps like Calm, Headspace, Classpass, Fitbit, Woebot, Talkspace, BetterHelp, and Virgin Pulse.

Let us look again at the work of Leena Nair when she was at Unilever – who can proudly boast a 250% return on investment on health and wellbeing.[37] They have trained 3,000 employees as mental health champions, engaged leaders in the narrative, and made wellbeing an official part of each employee's annual performance and development review.[38]

The impact on the company culture has been dramatic, according to Leena:

> *Employee engagement is through the roof. Pride in Unilever is in the high 90s... People really see Unilever is putting their wellbeing first, and that has a huge role to play in how engaged they are and how willing they are to go the extra mile.*[39]

The key is to understand the drivers of employee wellbeing in the context of your organisation through ongoing, two-way communication with employees. You need to understand their needs, wishes and sentiment towards different aspects of their job and workplace, then use this to show they have a voice, you have listened, and this has informed your own (and hence the organisation's) decisions, behaviours and actions towards them.

Professor Derek Mowbray has developed the concept and practice of Psychological Responsibility at work. He defines it as this:

> *Psychological Responsibility is a responsibility that organisations place on each individual in the workforce to remain psychologically well and to ensure they do no psychological harm to anyone else.*[40]

He goes on to say:

> *The implications include the expectation that individuals will alert their leaders and managers to any situation of circumstance where they feel their psychological wellbeing is being compromised by the demands made on them or the behaviour of others. It is part of the expectation that once a situation is identified, action is taken by the individual concerned to influence the event or behaviour or remove themselves from being exposed to the event or behaviour, or that their leader or manager takes action to prevent the event or behaviour from occurring.*[41]

This joint responsibility between individual and employer demonstrates how the world of work has evolved. Individuals, leaders and organisations have seen a shift towards being required to listen, show empathy, and look out for the wellbeing and health of themselves and their colleagues.

But this may not come naturally to some managers and leaders, they may need to be coached to understand business drivers and data, to understand the impact of behaviours and decisions on stress levels, absence and sickness or turnover. Do they know or care about the hours people are working? What does your data tell you, in terms of variations or patterns within different roles or locations? Are there different patterns across countries, age groups or genders? What is the impact on productivity among those who are working too much? Again, you have the opportunity to build a picture of a strategic need to be addressed, offer a solution, and then show demonstrable ROI from your efforts.

One heart-warming change over recent times has been that in many organisations we have heard more and more people taking a real interest in each other, asking sincere questions, such as: 'How are you? No, *really*, how are you?' Day-to-day, we see leaders and colleagues sharing their hopes and concerns with one another, showing care, and looking out for each others' wellbeing, in a way that was unusual or non-existent before. Co-workers now give and receive increased physical, mental, and emotional support during strange, unpredictable, and unsettling times. People have become more thoughtful, considerate, and kind. The more employees experience and are moved by their leader's compassion or kindness, the more loyal they become to the leader. As Seth Godin says in his book, *Tribes*, 'Humans beings can't help it, we need to belong.'[42] This sense of community-through-adversity gives people a sense of 'being in it together', which is essential if people are to be resilient.

Again, we see how evolution does not necessarily equate to improvement; we know you can get your work done at home, but (putting aside the issues with 'always on' culture we have already looked at) the office is where culture and community develops. In a hybrid workplace, if you have a large proportion of your people working away from the office – you will need to work closely with leaders to develop the sense of community and show the organisation cares.

It is difficult to look at the new hybrid, flexible mix of home and office working – where employees are given the opportunity to work where and when is most comfortable for them – and not conclude this is the best way to enhance productivity while preserving happiness through greater family time, and so on. But you need to be careful this doesn't come at the expense of the coherence of your organisational culture and all the great things that culture facilitates and delivers when people are brought together. It is when people spend time with the others, particularly those they don't know and who offer different perspectives, that share ideas and spark innovation and improvement. As such, the office is vital for maintaining and developing your organisational culture and creating a sense of community. As we saw at FedEx Express, you need to ensure there are touch points and learning opportunities at every turn, to ensure you maintain employees' engagement with your organisation, its purpose and goals.

CARE AND CONQUER

No matter where colleagues are based, it can be effective to champion wellbeing – and help ensure it becomes fully embedded in your culture. This fundamental duty of care in many leading organisations is also extended to their:

- communities (that your company works in and serves)
- partners
- consumers.

Business benefits naturally flow from fulfilling this duty of care and considerable trust and goodwill is built around their brands.

This was the approach beer maker AB InBev adopted during the pandemic, adopting the mantra of 'transitioning from what we know how to do, to what we can do'. As it sought to protect the wellbeing of its key stakeholders, the firm's key questions were:

- What are we good at?
- How can we play an expanded role?

InBev not only made sure colleagues had the best safety products and measures, and as up-to-date information as possible, but its leaders also refocused the organisation's manufacturing expertise towards making three million face masks and three million bottles of hand sanitiser. They also changed the terms on which they worked with their partners, from farmers to restaurant owners, to support them, as well as creating beer deliveries direct to consumers to help keep them entertained in lockdown. This was all delivered within a longer-term strategy to make sure beer would be part of the economic recovery, benefitting businesses right across the firm's supply chain.

This response was the right thing to do and it helped the company embed itself in that recovery. But at the root of it all was a desire to fulfil a duty of care to the wellbeing of those they felt responsible for and to. They were rewarded with something much better than short-term sales; this strategy garnered the firm greater trust and greater loyalty from its people, its suppliers and its customers, helping to ensure business success in the future. It is a powerful lesson for all organisations.

POSITIVE CULTURES AT WORK

We have seen companies successfully start movements designed to drive a positive workplace culture. When asked why they are doing it, they tell us that they want to ensure the workforce is psychologically fit, well, and happy. They are trying to create an environment where people play to their strengths, give and receive support and encouragement, and perform to the best of their abilities.

In her book *Positivity*, Professor Barbara Fredrickson defines the concept using ten specific traits: joy, gratitude, serenity, interest, hope, pride, amusement, inspiration, awe, and love.[43] It is no surprise that these same traits underpin some of the world's most inspirational organisations.

Fredrickson's research explores the science of positive mind-states and how they can help us bounce back from setbacks, make meaningful connections with others, and improve our health and happiness. Good feelings come and go, she argues. That is natural. The goal is to increase the amount of positivity you experience each day. Over time, these experiences add up and help build your physical, mental, and psychological wellbeing.

Fredrickson says that, in life, for every single negative experience we have, we should create at least three positive experiences to counteract the negative effects. In the workplace, she suggests that this ratio should even be closer to 5:1.

Her research shows that positivity has a 'tipping point'. The 3:1 positivity ratio may well be a magic number in human psychology. Once you reach a positivity tipping point, you create upward spirals in your life – or your organisational culture. Once you fall below the tipping point, you create downward spirals in your life or culture. As she notes: 'The consistency here is extraordinary. For individuals, marriages, and business teams who are flourishing or doing remarkably well, this comes with positivity ratios above 3:1.'

The key to encouraging this kind of positivity in the workplace is helping people to:

- play to their strengths
- give positive feedback where deserved
- perform acts of kindness or help others
- stop listening to negativity in the news or on social media
- challenge their beliefs which limit them and hold them back.

Listen to good news stories (from inside and outside the company). Ultimately, this will mean those working in your organisation find themselves surrounded by positive people who will support each other and form a deeper, more positive relationship with the company.

Positive work cultures naturally engender happier, more successful organisations. In his book *59 Seconds*, Richard Wiseman says, 'Happiness doesn't just flow from success; it actually causes it.'[44] Likewise, in *The Happiness Advantage* Shawn Achor says, 'We become more successful when we are happier and more positive, not the other way around.'[45]

Dr David R. Hamilton tells us that when people think positive thoughts they create a chemical change in their brain that releases serotonin, giving us a 'feel good' boost. People who feel good tend to perform well. Put in stark business terms, happiness will improve ROI across all sections of the business. This is a crucial lesson in 4IR[46] – a world characterised by increasing uncertainty and change. In this environment firms are going to have to pay greater attention to employee happiness and put greater effort into boosting and sustaining it.

With the advent of AI and machine working, it is even more important to remind ourselves that people are not robots. They are – and will remain for the near future – human. If we are to get the best out of them on behalf of the organisation we ultimately need to fulfil a core human aim, and that is happiness.

THE HAPPINESS FACTOR

An important way of improving our colleagues' sense of happiness at work is to understand and acknowledge their human needs. In their book *Primed to Perform*, Neel Doshi and Lindsay McGregor say creating positive cultures at work means creating an environment that meets human needs. By doing this, we enable people to perform at their best. When our needs are met, this makes us happy[47] – and happy employees, coupled with high performance, mean happy customers.

We see this in practice in research by Oxford University's Saïd Business School, in collaboration with British multinational telecoms firm BT. This paper demonstrated that happy employees saw a 'large increase in sales' compared to those subjected to 'gloomy weather'.[48]

In the words of one the study's authors, Professor Jan-Emmanuel De Neve:

> *We found that when workers are happier, they work faster by making more calls per hour worked and, importantly, convert more calls to sales.*[49]

But what really makes people happy?

The World Happiness Report surveys thousands of individuals in over 150 countries. The 2020 report showed that the number one driver for happiness is 'Social Support', defined by the relationships and sense of community individuals have in their lives. This variable was measured as being 6.4 times more important than wealth.[50]

The second most important driver was 'Freedom', which means that individuals can pursue the lives they wish to live.[51]

The data from the 2022 study indicates that leaders who aim to offer freedom and flexibility will observe happier employees and peers. These are powerful drivers of happiness and are a great place to start if you want to start building the core tenets of a happy, productive culture at your company. However, those wanting to delve deeper into the psychology of human need will find out more about addressing core human needs in the 'Purpose' section.

CASE STUDY: HOW ZAPPOS LEFT OTHER SHOEMAKERS STANDING

For a great example of a company that put happiness first and blew the opposition away, then you need look no further than Zappos.com. This online shoe and clothing shop, based in Las Vegas, launched into a highly competitive and well-established market in 1999. A mere ten years later, it was sold to Amazon for $1.2bn. Within eight years, the organisation turned $8m in sales into $1.2bn. Furthermore, across the sector, turnover rates are typically 150%, whereas Zappos has limited this to just 7%.[52, 53, 54]

Researchers from the University of Colorado looked into what had driven this extraordinary success and found that when the late Tony Hsieh became Zappos CEO, he focused on three principles[55]:

1. employee happiness
2. exceptional customer service
3. high performance.

All HR and learning and leadership was aligned to happiness and these core principles. This empowered staff to become aligned with a common purpose that they believed in and that they willingly strived to fulfil.[56]

This energy is embedded into each new member of staff from day one. Zappos only hires people who are willing to emulate, live, and breathe the core values of the organisation. When Zappos hires someone, new staff members undergo learning programs that explain how they are expected to meet the requirements of the culture.[57] At one point, the firm's cultural orientation programme offered any new starter who didn't want to buy in – no matter their role or seniority – $3,000 to leave if they were not happy.[58]

In his book, *Delivering Happiness*, Hsieh explains that this approach offered connectedness – a feeling of being part of an inclusive tribe – that made people happy and, in turn, created a sense of fulfilment. This culture was underpinned by openness, honesty, and feedback among staff, suppliers and customers.[59]

Zappos clearly demonstrates that when a group of people feels happy and connected there is a strong sense of obligation to the whole team, a desire to work harder and to treat each other better. In Zappo's case this went beyond simply feeling connected, it was about shared purpose and passions. Zappos' common purpose was simple: making customers happy – or, as the firm puts it: 'Deliver[ing] WOW through service'.[60] This goal was only achievable with exceptional customer service and fast, accurate delivery systems.

Hsieh rightly spotted that what brought this together was common purpose and, ultimately, happy employees. Creating those happy employees could not have happened without a strong company culture, formed by people who have a common goal and who were supported, maintained and developed by learning and leadership (driven by insights from all stakeholders). Hsieh knew the company's core values – coupled with great tech – would deliver happy, capable employees that would drive and strive to deliver the firm's goals – in Zappos' case, exceptional customer service. This is a great example of 4IR people and culture coming together with 4IR tech to create holistic service delivery.

HIGH-TRUST CULTURES

Building a high-trust culture, where employees feel trusted is not without its challenges. There are clear benefits of course: people are more productive, they are more energised and engaged, they collaborate better with their colleagues, and stay with the business longer. Unfortunately, we live in a time where trust seems increasingly difficult to come by.

The *Edelman Trust Barometer 2022*, by the communications firm of the same name, measures trust levels across many institutions, sectors and geographical regions. The Barometer surveys more than 34,000 respondents across 28 countries. Their key findings included:

- 42% trust government
- 46% trust journalists
- 49% trust CEOs
- Nearly 60% say their default tendency is to distrust something until they see evidence it is trustworthy.[61]

There is clearly a challenge here, but there is also a tremendous opportunity. Let us look at the low trust issue from a different angle. Technological advancements mean people are far less accepting of traditional hierarchies, orthodoxies, and sources of information today. They no longer blindly trust everything they read and hear in the media. People are holding politicians to account more frequently. The technological age in which we live means we are more likely to go out and find things out for ourselves. In this scenario, we could say the trust we previously put in different people and institutions was misplaced in the first place, because of an information deficit.

That information deficit is now closing, and our levels of trust are being set at a more accurate and realistic level. Of course, there is a real chance of us drowning in information, with at least some of it false or being maliciously employed. But the simple fact is we are seeking truth like never before. Yes, our trust in certain elements of society may have diminished, but our desire to trust and be trusted has never gone away. Organisations should see this as a great chance to build trust with all their stakeholders – not just their staff – and differentiate themselves and the way they do business.

So why is trust so important? In simple terms, trust increases joy and engagement. Neuroscience has shown the brain generates oxytocin – also known as 'the love drug'[62] – when we feel we are trusted, reducing any fears we might be feeling and increasing our happiness.[63] So, we naturally feel better when we feel trusted, but the benefits don't stop there. As the neurological state that trust promotes reduces any fear we might be feeling, it also increases the clarity with which we think (as our 'fight or flight' mechanism is suppressed). In turn, we make better decisions and are more productive. It is a virtuous circle.

In his book *The Speed of Trust*, Stephen M. R. Covey and Rebecca R. Merrill write that trust always affects two measurable outcomes: speed and cost.[64] When trust goes down – whether that be in a relationship with a colleague or customer, in a team, a company, or across a wider industry – speed decreases with it. Everything takes longer, and the consequence is costs increase. Conversely, when trust goes up, speed goes up with it and cost comes down. Everything happens faster and everything costs less because trust has been established.

So, what drives trust? The answer is simple; it is based on:

- honesty
- transparency
- freedom
- collaboration.

High-trust cultures can typically be described as inclusive environments where everyone feels valued as an individual. You will see regular private and public recognition of high performance (although, interestingly, it is often more important for staff to be recognised by their peers). These organisations encourage and reward collaboration and building of new relationships, as part of a culture of continuous learning. Knowledge is shared and conversations are open and, crucially, people are clear about what is expected of them.

As they are clear on those expectations, leaders feel safe to empower their staff to make decisions, deliver their work in the way they feel is best, and undertake challenging projects designed to develop their experiences and skills. At the same time, colleagues feel safe to ask for help and admit they don't know an answer.

Another crucial aspect of that empowerment is giving staff a voice and ensuring they are listened to and their feedback and ideas are valued and actioned. The John Lewis Partnership, a leading UK retailer, offers a strong example of employee voice in action. What's amazing is their employee-centric model has been in place for almost 100 years. In 1929, John Spedan Lewis relinquished his possession of the firm so that the employees of tomorrow could lead his 'experiment in industrial democracy'.[65] His ideas are set out in the company's constitution, which aims to create a 'better form of business'.[66]

The 80,000 staff who work for John Lewis as of June 2022, including those at their department stores and supermarkets are called 'partners'. They are also the firm's owners. As the organisation says: 'Partners share in the benefits and profits of a business that puts them first'.[67] To help make this a reality, the three governance organs that run John Lewis benefit from the input of more than 3,000 elected representatives.[68] This all means that partners have a real stake in decision-making, challenge management on performance, and have a vocal say in how the business operates. This was demonstrated when Executive Director for People, Lisa Cherry joined and her first thought when planning to shape the future of John Lewis was to spend time with partners to properly understand the business.

If you can promote behaviour, systems and processes that reflect these elements in your workplace, you will see the returns quickly.

Speaking of returns, let us go back to that all-important issue of business ROI to help you justify your efforts in this area. In organisations characterised as having high trust:

- Turnover rates are around 50% less than at rival organisations.[69]
- There is 50% higher productivity than in 'low-trust' competitors.[70]
- Stock market returns are around two to three times higher than the industry average.[71]
- There are 13% fewer sick days.[72]

To put it another way:

high trust =
greater productivity +
increased return to shareholders

That increased return to shareholders is indicative of the greater levels of customer satisfaction reported in those firms as well.

If you're looking to take a first step on the road to a high-trust culture, it is worth turning to Dr Amy Cuddy of Harvard University, who has done extensive research into high-trust organisations. She says a powerful driver in building trust amongst employees is for leaders to first demonstrate trust in them. Employees who feel trusted are more likely to feel empowered and more likely to feel engaged and happy with their role. They are more likely to trust, collaborate with, and commit to their leaders.

Workplace consultancy Great Places to Work has identified seven distinct ways organisations build high-trust cultures. These steps are:[73]

1. Identify and invest your workforce in your organisational purpose.
2. Have faith in and facilitate your staff's performance.
3. Listen to your workers.
4. Help your employees understand the benefit their work has on customers.
5. Build a work family.

6. Reward staff for the value they add.
7. Adopt a culture of 'giving back' to the community.

The companies we have been working with to implement our CAPEX formula consciously and deliberately promote these behaviours, creating positive habits and ways of working. They know that high-trust cultures have lower rates of stress and talent attrition, and higher levels of well-being and engagement. The high levels of trust they built lead to high performance. Once again, we are talking about them making a positive impact on the bottom line for their business.

It is worth noting that one of the most challenging – and pivotal – of Great Place to Work's seven steps (above), is defining your company's purpose and connecting people to it. We're talking about understanding, crafting and communicating your firm's own unique narrative – The Story of Us – to your colleagues and building a community around that messaging. This is tough, and for that reason, later in this book, we will look in depth at how you can bring the vision for your organisation and the profession to life, and then embed it. There, we will help you tell the story you want to tell to the people who need to hear it. We will also explain the key principles to building a movement that will support, embrace, and drive that purpose forward, using the organisational culture that will bring it to life.

ADDITIONAL FIGURES

Employee turnover rates are around 50% lower than industry competitors:[74]

- Stock market returns are two to three times higher than average.
- High-trust cultures are connected to greater levels of customer satisfaction.

Compared to people at low-trust companies, people at high-trust companies report:[75]

- 74% less stress
- 106% more energy at work
- 50% higher productivity
- 13% fewer sick days
- 76% more engagement
- 29% more satisfaction with their lives
- 40% less burnout.

CAPEX – 'A' IS FOR ADAPTABILITY

We have looked at how organisational culture provides a bedrock on which all your company's activities should take place. But we must be careful not to interpret culture – and its role as a guiding light in how you do business – as something restrictive. Culture will give you the wider context, but the ability to take that context and adapt and thrive within it will be crucial to success in the Fourth Industrial Revolution (4IR). Let us remind ourselves of how Klaus Schwab – who popularised the moniker – differentiated this phenomenon from the digital changes we've been seeing since the 1960s (the Third Industrial Revolution). Schwab noted:

> *There are three reasons why today's transformations represent not merely a prolongation of the Third Industrial Revolution but rather the arrival of a Fourth and distinct one: velocity, scope, and systems impact. The speed of current breakthroughs has no historical precedent.*[76]

In this environment, adaptability will be key to thriving, both in terms of organisational process and structures, and in terms of people and how they approach day-to-day challenges. This ability to adapt will come from an agility that can only exist through collaboration and cooperation. Businesses that grasp this will move away from rigid structures, strategies and tactics, towards a state of constant readiness. They will have the ability to learn from their mistakes, bounce back from setbacks, and be prepared for a range of possible outcomes.

> *You cannot step twice into the same stream.*
> *~Socrates' account of Heraclitus (b. 544 BCE) philosophy*[77]

Avil Beckford's take on this ancient quote shines a valuable light for our purposes:

> *For me, the river is always moving because it's alive, so it's never the same.*[78]

You can bake adaptability into your organisation through your learning strategies. Put bluntly, the capacity and capability that people have to learn determines their capacity and capability to adapt. Getting the right learning strategies in place can be beneficial in multiple ways. You will of course prepare the company to react quickly and effectively in rapidly changing environments, but this will only come if you enable colleagues to develop skills that keep them relevant and increase their employability, in turn deepening the connection between them and the company.

That is why creating an environment where learning is central to the corporate culture – where it is woven into the fabric of business decisions – will help build an organisation that can adapt and, by its very nature, be more innovative and more likely to succeed.

Another pitfall we must avoid is fear of change. Of course, we've all heard that people fear change, but it tends not to be true if change is well managed. What people really fear is the *idea* of change. They fear the uncertainty. They fear moving out of their comfort zone. When change happens, it can be quite the opposite of what they expected. It can be refreshing, invigorating, and empowering – but only if people are equipped with the skills and mindset to ride that wave.

You will need to make sure people are comfortable with the notion of uncertainty and give them the support they need to approach this era of flux with confidence. In 4IR you must ensure learning is a continuous journey that instils the notion that success will be built on how we handle what we don't know, as much as it will turn on what we do. Put another way, you must make learning a habit that matters to people. It must be a habit that exists to solve business problems and develop future-critical skills that unlock and enable business performance.

With any luck you will be pleasantly surprised by how aware people are of the 'new normal' you are looking to cater for, and how much they will value your ability to prepare them for an adaptable future. Hybrid working has offered many people a crash course in adaptability and, at the same time, revealed not just that they could change, but how quickly they could and would adapt when necessity demanded it. The idea of organisations becoming resilient and agile through adaptability has been forced on everyone in a way and at a speed that would have been impossible otherwise.

When the COVID-19 outbreak began, many organisations went through more change in a few weeks than they had done for years. They found that people could learn and evolve in all sorts of ways, in terms of their habits, beliefs and skills. Pharmaceutical firm Novartis had a two-year plan to roll out Microsoft Teams. The pandemic saw it execute the programme in two weeks.[79] This included transferring 60,000 people to remote working over one weekend.[80]

In this chapter we will look at what it takes to foster an environment that will make this kind of adaptability second nature to a business and its people, rather than being something forced on it by sudden and unexpected changes.

It is perfectly possible to build adaptability into your organisation in a planned and orderly way. To do this, there are three cornerstones of adaptability that you need to consider:

- **Structure**: your organisational design and systems needs to evolve to be fluid and adaptive, driven by systems that are simple and connected.
- **Skills**: the talents we have prioritised and developed in the past are likely not what we need for the future; you will need to focus on building digital capacity that can drive critical (connected) thinking, creativity, problem solving, and innovation.
- **Behaviour**: you need to encourage flexibility in your colleagues' outlooks and actions and be prepared to put in the time to help them learn, reflect, and develop.

Let us go into each of these in more detail.

THE FIRST CORNERSTONE OF ADAPTABILITY: STRUCTURE

TEAMS FIT FOR 4IR

Transforming team performance is one the biggest opportunities for learning professionals in the new world of work. There are big changes afoot in how teams are seen and how they operate in 4IR. The nature of this new era demands adaptability is baked into our working systems and structures. Rigid teams are a major barrier to that, and you need to be asking how you can support and facilitate much greater flexibility.

Martin Whitehouse, Head of Future Capabilities at British American Tobacco, says this is the time for learning, using the skills required for the future to be the guiding principle for organisational design. This sentiment is echoed by Melanie Hayes, Chief People Officer at Harvey Nash Group, 'learning's role is to work with the business to create an agile organisation and to develop the skills to ensure you will be fit for the future'.

You'll no doubt have noted more *ad hoc* teams or groupings coming together and breaking up within your organisation, based on matching the right people to the business challenge. This approach was pioneered through the 'agile' approach to software development, which is based on iterative development, where requirements and solutions evolve through collaboration between self-organising cross-functional teams. It encourages teamwork, self-organisation and accountability, as well as aligning outputs with customer needs and company goals. There is also crossover with principles of the 'lean' approach, developed in manufacturing. This is a process of continuous improvement techniques and activities, which define 'waste' as anything that doesn't add value to the customer.

'Surge' or 'swarm teams' are one manifestation of this new way of working that is spreading beyond niche areas and into the mainstream. These agile team structures enable teams to form and dissolve quickly to deal with whatever the matter is at hand. As this strategy matures we will see the correct person leading the team, regardless of position, global location or length of service.

These teams will be naturally inclusive and embrace diversity in its widest sense, from neuro- or cognitive diversity, to diverse genders, races, and so on. The people involved in such structures know they will get a better solution by including people who are there simply because they *are the right people* to have on board. Such a grouping maximises the chance of success in solving any given problem and then delivering the solution, while also developing participants' experiences, skills and employability.

This new form of adaptable working will require more access from a greater number of people to senior leaders for quick decision-making. It will require a culture where you can grab a moment to speak to whoever you want (presuming your questions are to the relevant people). To make this work, colleagues will need to take more personal responsibility and accountability for their performance, scope of work and their learning. The organisation will need to empower them to make decisions themselves, having had the opportunity to collaborate with others and gauge multiple perspectives.

Indeed, surge teams are just the tip of the 4IR iceberg. They are a symptom of a wider trend towards a flexible organisational design that promotes alternative networks and self-managed teams; where autonomous, multi-disciplinary teams are increasingly responsible for their own direction. There are sound business reasons for this: it leads to increased adaptability, collaboration and a more entrepreneurial mindset. But it won't work if people do not have the skills and knowledge required to pull this off.

Plenty of firms have or are implementing systems to embed this adaptability.

At any one time, Coca-Cola's Latin America operation has 30% of the firm's teams focused on strategic objectives and strategies, new products and new ways of working to drive innovation. This happens in teams that are formed to meet a strategic objective and disband once that objective is met. The other 70% of the business operates in a traditional manner and structure to deliver operations and production.

Spotify has a structure of autonomous 'Squads', where they trust people and teams to make informed decisions about the way they work.[81] These teams account for about a third of the firm's organisational headcount, a model that allows greater flexibility and agility. They are built on an agile philosophy that seeks continuous improvement, both for the individual and in the wider organisation.[82] The other two-thirds of the organisation is based on a traditional hierarchy and focused mainly on support functions.

This is not just a Western model. We find similar examples all over the world. Haier is a Chinese manufacturer and the world's top home appliance producer, with 70,000 employees.[83] The firm has taken out its entire middle management level, creating an ecosystem of teams where senior leaders still set the direction and strategy, but in which the teams have become small companies connected via an online platform. This structure has given employees greater ownership of their work and inspired an 'entrepreneurial' mindset.[84] It also means they have the flexibility to use their talents to meet the needs of the future of work.[85]

It is worth noting that such flexibility also applies to your teams collaborating with their competitors – something that might have been counterintuitive just a few years ago, but which is critical to a successful business today. The fact organisations now regularly work together with competing and non-competing partners to co-brand or bring new products and services to market is a fantastic example of flexibility in action. Examples we can look to include:

- Pfizer and Merck: these pharma companies have entered a strategic partnership to bring new cancer treatments to the market as soon as possible.[86]
- Vimeo and YouTube: their collaboration allows Vimeo creators to publish their videos to YouTube.

- Uber and Spotify: Uber passengers can play their own music in taxis cars, offering an enhanced travel experience that also encourages those without Spotify to download the app.[87]
- GoPro and Red Bull: one sells high-grade portable cameras, the other energy drinks. Both have established themselves as lifestyle brands for the adventurous and these shared values make them a perfect pairing for co-branding campaigns and collaborating on events.[88]

At the centre of this whole flexible mantra is collaboration. Without it, the benefits will not be realised. Scott Page is an expert in organisational complexity at the University of Michigan. He notes that artificial intelligence offers a similar lesson. AI is not about single algorithms; it is a team of algorithms that look at the search differently to find the optimal solution to the problem. This is exactly the way our teams can thrive as a collective, based on their varied experiences.[89] In this way they can harness different perspectives, build connections, and in turn increase their ability to learn through trial and error during a period of rapid change and uncertainty.

This means learning professionals focusing on creating opportunities for colleagues to collaborate, developing the ability of the individual to adapt and take on new roles efficiently and quickly. Focusing on the dual outcome of solving business problems, and giving people the experiences they need to develop for the future.

TAKE THE COMPLEXITY OUT

The nature of 4IR demands simplicity. You'll no doubt have noticed yourself how many more tasks you have to do these days – and how much less time you have to get things done. Technology has exponentially increased the speed at which we can do things but, as we keep seeing, its application tends to forget the human beings responsible for reaping the actual value of these super-charged processes.

In their book *Six Simple Rules,* Yves Morieux and Peter Tollman of the Boston Consulting Group (BCG), lay out the reasons the world of work is getting so much more complex. There are:[90]

- more stakeholders with demands
- more customers with more choices
- more markets home and abroad
- more requirements
- more conflicting demands
- faster change than ever before.

Morieux and Tollman cite BCG's Complexity Index, which shows complexity has risen six-fold since 1955. [91] In the top 20% of complicated organisations, managers spend more than 40% of their time writing reports and between 30% and 60% of their total work hours in meetings. Amazingly BCG shows the average number of procedures in these large organisations goes up by 6.7% per year, so they have a 35-fold increase in the 55 years they have been studying it. They suggest fewer systems, more flexibility and autonomy, and rewarding cooperation and collaboration.

Something has to give as technology becomes more readily available to anyone who wishes to have it. If you're not careful, your technology will overpromise and your people will underdeliver because they are so busy, they simply can't adapt fast enough. We cannot and *must* not confuse back-to-back meetings with being productive. To make sure this doesn't happen, the learning professional will need to support the organisation's leaders in applying a simple mantra wherever possible: simplify, simplify, simplify. That means simplifying processes, simplifying language and simplifying priorities.

The key to making this work is to ensure everyone knows what they're doing and what adds value. Unnecessary process or hierarchy slows down decision-making and is a massive barrier to the speed of innovation and adaptability. If we are to adapt and thrive in this new world of fluid work we need to simplify, simplify, simplify.

THE SECOND CORNERSTONE OF ADAPTABILITY: SKILLS

THE RIGHT SKILLS FOR AN ADAPTABLE FUTURE

The skills that your colleagues will need to adapt and thrive in the Fourth Industrial Revolution are changing. It is not just digital capabilities that are changing at breakneck speed and where upskilling and reskilling are vital. Having analysed research from numerous organisations, including McKinsey[92], the Harvard Business Review[93], Deloitte[94], and the World Economic Forum[95], we consider the top five skills that will be required among employees to make any organisation thrive are:

1. creativity and critical (connected) thinking
2. resilience and the ability to navigate through uncertainty
3. collaboration and building trust
4. complex problem solving and decision-making
5. influence and persuasion.

Your learning structures, processes and programs will need to address all these core skillsets if you want to play a strategic role in future-proofing your organisation. You also need to think of these five holistically, since they are interconnected.

CREATIVITY AND CRITICAL (CONNECTED) THINKING

The first of these key skills – critical (or 'connected') thinking – will perhaps be the most unfamiliar, certainly among the wider swathe of your colleagues. But it is crucial because an increasing focus on innovation and productivity, driven by technological changes, will require ever-greater creativity. To unlock this spark we will need to teach and develop our colleagues in being able to find patterns and notice trends in information and ideas. Innovators tend to explain connected thinking in terms of joining up or connecting the dots. They use it to find hidden patterns and make connections that other people do not see, often in seemingly unrelated things.

This trait is not new. It has existed throughout history. Leonardo da Vinci, for example, defined innovation as connecting the unconnected – something he was particularly good at. His expertise in anatomy helped him to create better sculptures and portraits and make sense of mechanics and engineering. But only now is there a widespread demand for it in the workplace. We will look at this skill in more detail and its impact on learning in the X-Factor section (and look a bit more at how Leonardo did it so well).

RESILIENCE AND THE ABILITY TO NAVIGATE THROUGH UNCERTAINTY

Resilience is a factor we have mentioned numerous times already. Workers are going to have to show plenty of this to bounce back from set backs and learn as they deal with a lot of change and uncertainty, whilst, at the same time, remaining positive. This will mean looking after both their own wellbeing and that of others.

COLLABORATION AND BUILDING TRUST

This notion of looking out for others extends into how people and teams work together. For creativity to flourish, people will need to collaborate increasingly closely. This will require building high-trust environments and high-performance cultures that will become the foundations of true innovation.

COMPLEX PROBLEM SOLVING AND DECISION-MAKING

If the kinds of environments we mention above are to survive and flourish, we are going to have to solve some complex problems and make tough decisions quickly. For this to happen we need to harness the collective intelligence of our colleagues by using connected thinking and diversity in its widest sense. In the connected world it is naive to think only one person – or even a certain group of people – has the answer.

INFLUENCE AND PERSUASION

In 4IR, we will see many new skills needed, but one area where traditional skills will remain of importance is the ability to influence and persuade. As we've seen, this era will demand greater trust within organisations. One manifestation of that will be colleagues having the ability and the courage to stand-up, have a voice and be heard (and for the organisation to listen too). This means the art of persuasion will be as important as ever, with the ability to tell an evidenced-based story to influence others increasing in value. These will need to be underpinned by emotional intelligence and the ability to apply social influence.

But, while these skills are not new, the big difference will be that they can no longer be limited to people in formal leadership positions, they are now required by everyone. It will be your job to help ensure these skills are developed throughout the business, and that the culture of openness and trust exists, where everyone can make the best use of them.

LEADERSHIP

It is unrealistic for a leader to know everything, particularly in a time of rapid change. In response to this, dynamic organisations have adopted a belief that leadership capability should be distributed throughout the organisation and be part of every employee's skill set.

There's no better place to look for direction on this kind of leadership model than James P. Spillane's book *Distributed Leadership*[96] and Jon Ingham's work, *The Social Organization.*[97] They developed the idea that leadership is a behaviour and mindset, not a role. They believe it should be systemic and developed and influenced by everyone at all levels of the organisation. The benefits of distributed leadership include:

- greater responsiveness to customer/market requirements
- improved quality of decision making, i.e., leads to stronger sense of ownership
- more entrepreneurialism that generates more initiatives and ideas
- improved levels of motivation and enthusiasm.

The importance of this distributed leadership approach is growing as organisations lean on communities and networks as much as functional teams to get things done. The 'surge' teams we've already mentioned are an example of this. They pull together disparate groups of people for a specific task and then break up afterwards. This organic – and highly effective – approach simply can't work if traditional groupings, hierarchies, and silos are maintained.

The challenge is to breed leadership traits within everyone, rather than a management cadre – and to start doing it as early as possible. If, as most companies do, your business has a more structured and hierarchical notion of leadership, your company's values and culture are going to be seriously put to the test as 4IR continues. The first-time corporate manager generally attains this position at approximately 30 years old. Frighteningly, the average age at which they then start on leadership training schemes is forty-two, according to Jack Zenger in the *Harvard Business Review*.[98] But the nature of work in the future means promotions are going to happen earlier and earlier in people's careers to enable businesses to be more fluid and adaptable to rapidly changing circumstances. It is up to you to empower colleagues so they have the capacity to step up when circumstances demand it. Leadership training schemes cannot wait for someone to already be in their forties. If it is not too late already, it certainly will be in years to come.

NORTHAMPTONSHIRE HEALTHCARE NHS FOUNDATION TRUST (NHFT)

The CAPEX code is being used in the world's leading organisations, as well as the innovative brands and disrupters. But the formula is also working in more traditional settings – and settings don't come much bigger and more traditional than the UK's National Health Service (NHS).

The NHS is the single biggest employer in the UK, with 1.7m workers across England, Wales, Scotland and Northern Ireland.[99] This also makes it the fifth-largest workforce in the world.[100] The NHS is a much-loved organisation, but endures constant challenges around and stemming from funding, care delivery, staffing, political interference, poor management, and a host of other issues.

As such, the Northamptonshire Trust has suffered from many ailments, as does the Service right across the board. In 2016, the Trust had significant challenges in terms of finances, quality and efficiency. The results of the *NHS National Staff Survey* (2016) for NHFT were not pretty.[101] They showed that both the proportion of staff recommending the Trust as a place to work and the Trust's overall staff engagement score were falling. This was contributing to a significant vacancy rate, which was hitting the Trust's finances, quality and efficiency due to it relying on agency staff. These results, along with a rating of 'Requires Improvement' from the Care Quality Commission (CQC),[102] highlighted that NHFT needed to improve the experience of staff and help them feel empowered and valued. It hoped this would, in turn, result in improved patient care and outcomes. But turning this around would be enormously tough, which made the successes it enjoyed – both financially and culturally – nigh-on miraculous.

WHAT THE TRUST DID

It focused on promoting distributed leadership, creating a culture change where the organisation's adaptability increased as did the engagement of the workforce. This new model was one where all staff regardless of role or band are treated, and expected to behave, as a leader.

The process began with an asking and listening exercise, where over 600 staff across the organisation were asked to consider times that they were well-led, and what this looked and felt like. This helped them build a model of what distributed leadership could and should look like in their context.

To develop the necessary skills, a distributed leadership mindset was embedded into learning programmes, workshops and conferences, as well as systems and processes. This mindset encouraged everyone to:

- see themselves as leaders
- harness the potential of all staff and empower them to take personal responsibility for their work
- work more closely with colleagues to improve the outcomes for both service users and staff as a whole.

This focus quickly yielded successful outcomes for the Trust, including an 'Outstanding' rating from the CQC in 2018[103] and turning an almost £1.4m deficit[104] into a £4.1m surplus, per their 2018/19 report,[105] helping them provide even better healthcare.

A NEW PARADIGM

The only way to get the ball rolling on spreading distributed leadership is to engage your employees, explain the importance of this concept at all levels of the organisation, and put them at the forefront of this drive for adaptability.

But these leadership activities and outputs must also be matched by appropriate leadership styles. We're not just talking about the traditional issue of micro-managing colleagues who find themselves in positions of responsibility; we're talking about specific styles that are appropriate for 4IR.

Leaders will need to deliver their outcomes in a different way to before. Among the firms that are adapting quickly to this new era, a new and prevalent style of leadership is emerging that is rooted in authenticity. Being authentic allows us to connect with people more easily and makes it easier for us to perform at our best. It is hard trying to be someone you are not; it drains lots of our energy and takes away our focus. This is why ensuring that organisational values and purpose align with our own values and purpose is so important; and is something we will delve into in 'Purpose'.

In this new paradigm, a leader must be supported by learning professionals to:

- Understand their purpose and help others find theirs.
- Behave with honesty and be true to themselves, their values and their purpose. This means bringing their whole self to work, not just the bits that seem relevant to the role.
- Know who they are, where they are going, how they are going to get there, and why.
- Continuously learn through understanding their strengths, weaknesses and areas for development.

These parameters ask a lot of leaders. They demand a certain vulnerability that they might not be used to. But times have changed. Having the courage to be vulnerable and to admit we don't know all the answers is often seen as a strength – and it is helpful in building trust.

Of course, this can't be a free-for-all. Leaders must still set boundaries and should never appear to be simply soliciting sympathy through their vulnerability. People still want their tribe to have a leader. They still want to feel like there is a decisive hand on the tiller, a reassuring hand on the wheel. What they need to know now is the true nature of that guiding hand.

The authenticity we are talking about creates engagement and trust with a workforce, but it also has some practical drivers. In the era of 4IR we are going to have to network, learn and collaborate like never before. It is through these interactions we start to notice the patterns and trends that drive more informed strategic decision-making, reduce levels of uncertainty, and become agile in our choices. Without leaders who act as authentic, transparent role models, and who are the embodiment of the behaviour and values expected of the business, it will be difficult to create this innovative and creative environment.

Conversely, if your leaders develop leadership throughout the organisation through a distributed model, they will find it easier to collaborate across the business and solve complex business problems because they will be connecting with a far greater and more diverse range of people.

CASE STUDY: LEGO PLAYGROUND

Lego's transformative leadership programme was instigated in 2018, at a time of great change for the company. The retail landscape was changing fast. Toys "R" Us had collapsed, just as ecommerce rivals were seeing their sales go off the charts. Lego too had seen its sales stall. Something had to change. Leadership was needed – and not necessarily of the traditional kind.

But change was easier said than done. Not only was the firm suffering from the legacy of a deeply engrained hierarchical structure, its leadership framework was bafflingly complicated. An aspiring leader needed to process and execute strategic priorities, step up principles, leadership guardrails, a competency and proficiency framework, and even 'neuro indicators', which included 'Lego over ego'. As Patrick Curry, Head of Partnering & Operations, put it:

> *Holy cow were we overwhelming people. We needed to simplify our message on what leadership could and should look like at Lego.*

WHAT LEGO DID

First, the firm accepted things couldn't keep going the way they were. They realised there had been an underinvestment in technology and changing roles meant a traditional model of leadership – where the Sales VP of 25 years' experience was the go-to for all the answers – was no longer relevant.[106]

Lego got the ball rolling with the creation of a working group made up of 18 people, none of whom were part of the executive leadership team (but which included three representatives from HR). The membership represented all of the company's geographies, from Asia to China, and

Europe to America. This group was tasked with gathering insights from Lego colleagues around:

- What does Lego leadership look like to you?
- What does it feel like to work at Lego?
- What should we aspire to?

While the new strategy was not to be the brainchild of the executive leadership (instead they empowered the working group to come up with their own solutions), guidance was provided, including key design principles, such as:

1. It had to be rooted in the Lego brand framework (including its core values of imagination, creativity, fun, learning, caring and quality).
2. It had to be new (repackaging of the old wasn't acceptable).
3. It had to be the voice of Lego and speak to everyone.
4. It had to be a model for all Lego employees; it had to be leadership for all.
5. It had to be sustainable, lasting at least five years.

Over eight months, the team reviewed the evidence and many different leadership models before coming up with a solution: The Leadership Playground. This strategy has, as its core, the notion that leadership isn't a position, it is an act; a way of doing things that brings out the best in everybody. The model promotes three key leadership behaviours:

1. Be Brave.
2. Be Curious.
3. Be Focused.

Everyone in the company is then tasked with creating the conditions that enable those behaviours to unfold. By doing so, leaders – in whatever capacity – will fulfil the core goal to 'Energise Everyone Everyday'. As Lego says in its recruitment materials: 'By living these behaviours here, you'll be inspired to deliver your best – and you'll inspire others to do the same'.

The Playground is, in the words of CEO Niels B. Christiansen, a place where 'there is room for everyone to influence and empower and do stuff'[107]. Which takes us to the heart of this strategy: empowerment.

> *None of us like to be micro managed, we are all individuals with a strong mind and want to be influential in what we are doing,' says Niels. 'If you are busy with something you can be influential on it and you can see the results and feel accountable... the satisfaction of that is way higher... that is the energy that we need to tap into.*

To deliver the programme, 850 'Playground builders' were recruited from amongst the staff – one for each team – whose job it was to spread the message and promote practical activities that would help embed the programme. This included instigating 'camp fires', where colleagues could get together to chat about anything they wanted. They also encouraged the idea of 'missions'; micro programmes to solve problems that are driven by one of the three key behaviours.

> *You might work on focus and say if you are struggling with time management, set timers for each of your objectives, keep that focus,' Patrick explains. 'Or maybe with video updates for the brave mission, delete a meeting and send an update on a video instead... be brave... find out what happens.*

A year into the programme, the annual employee survey showed impressive results around adoption of the Lego Playground by respondents' colleagues and managers. The firm then focused on embedding the playground into the company's DNA, using 30–40 community builders who helped drive the Playground ethos forward and keep teams energised. This approach speaks, once again, to the underlying principle that leadership cannot just be driven top down, but must amplify experiences from across the organisation if leadership is to be something everyone is responsible for.

THE THIRD CORNERSTONE OF ADAPTABILITY: BEHAVIOUR

From as soon as 2033, 'born-mobile' employees will have always-on devices capable of providing simultaneous access to home and work life at any time. In a sci-fi-like turn, these may even be embedded under the skin.[108,109] Roles will emerge and disappear; they will be created by, and replaced by technology. We all need to prepare and act now – and that means more than learning new skills, we need to start *thinking and behaving differently*. Learning professionals need to step up to make sure it happens. Otherwise, the more than a third of people who say they are already anxious about the future and the impact of automation on their job may be the tip of the iceberg.[110]

Fortunately, the brain is exceptional at adjusting to new circumstances – a phenomenon known as neuroplasticity.[111] In other words, the brains in your colleagues' heads are naturally inclined towards aiding you in this process of behavioural change. At the same time, it is also important to realise that changing and embedding behaviour isn't easy. It takes time and it takes persistence. However, if you invest that time and effort, the pay-off will be huge.

The reason we say this is because we need to build adaptability and resilience into our mindsets. We want our people to be curious and want to learn, that is why parents, teachers and leaders often love and dread the question *'why?'* – it both shows the curiosity to learn but it may also cause an interruption when you are busy and may force you to look at things differently. In her book, *The Growth Mindset,* Carol Dweck explains that the people who learn best are not discouraged by failure – they don't even think they are failing. They think they are learning.[112] We need to teach, encourage and cajole people into thinking this way if they are to thrive in 4IR.

BUILDING SKILLS AND CHANGING BEHAVIOURS

Why does learning new skills and behavioural change take time? The answer lies in the science of brain function. As a brief overview, this shows that long-term memories can be made more reliable if we incorporate new information gradually and repeat it in timed intervals. The same rules apply to habits and behavioural change. A human being's skills, abilities and behaviours are not carved in stone and can be honed and changed, as long as it is done in a gradual and sustained way.

Let us return to the concept of neuroplasticity – the term that describes our brains' uncanny capacity to adjust. Scientists have shown that parts of our adult brains stay as malleable as a baby's, just like Plasticine.[113] Hopefully this puts the term 'neuroplasticity' into an easily graspable context. In essence, we can form fresh neural pathways that enable us to learn new things throughout our lives.[114] In practical terms, this means that what you do, practice, learn, and experience in life actually physically changes what your brain looks like. You are capable of rewiring your own brain and – by extension – capable of influencing learning and behaviour in others. This means that the key to changing behaviour and making it stick is good old-fashioned effort and willpower. This is particularly important if you hope to gain expertise in anything.

In *Habit*, pioneering philosopher and psychologist William James says the key to sustaining positive change is to use your willpower to turn each desired action into a habit, so that it comes automatically, without much effort, thought, or choice. In his words, creating good habits is the result of 'daily strokes of effort'.[115]

There are 3 types of willpower, as outlined by Kelly McGonigal at Stanford University:[116]

- **'I won't'**: A commitment to consciously resist or stop a behaviour or habit. This is the hardest approach to adopt for many people.
- **'I will'**: A commitment to take actions that may be uncomfortable, but are important in reaching your goals. This approach is about delayed gratification – shouldering a cost in return for benefits and rewards later. This is different from 'I won't' because you are putting a new behaviour in the place of an old behaviour (rather than just stopping something) and makes change easier. But it still takes a lot of energy and will power and, like a muscle, can get exhausted over time.
- **'I want to'**: A commitment to embrace the new and the different. This is the greatest form of willpower and the best way to energise behavioural change. It gives you a clear purpose, helping you embrace the new and the different. It is a great driver of adaptability because it focuses on purpose: the '*why?*' It gives you reason and it fulfils a need. It increases your passion, commitment and your belief in yourself and your goals. In turn, it increases your resilience in the face of difficulties, enabling you to sustain the changes you are making.

This effectiveness of this latter form of willpower is why having organisational cultures where people have a voice and are trusted to make decisions is so important to creating an agile organisation. When people 'want to' they are more resilient and can change more easily.

If you can instil the 'want to' mindset in yourself and your colleagues then the key to seeing practical results is to focus on changing one behaviour at a time. As the Russian proverb so adroitly puts it, 'If you chase two rabbits, you will not catch either one.'

To make it all a little bit easier and enjoyable, it is worth remembering that the act of being positive and happy is a good aid. In his book *The Happiness Advantage,* Shaun Achor notes that being happy and positive helps us organise new information, keep that information in the brain longer, and retrieve it faster later. In turn, we can make and sustain more neural connections; allowing us to:

- think more quickly and creatively
- become more skilled at complex analysis and problem solving
- see and invent new ways of doing things.[117]

If you encourage a culture of positivity and happiness among those you are helping to develop, behavioural change will come and faster and last longer.

FROM BEGINNER TO EXPERT

We are in a world of rapid change, so here's a big question: how long does it take to learn a new skill and to adopt a new behaviour (and so keep up)?

GETTING SKILLS UP TO SPEED

In terms of learning skills, that time period depends on how far you want to go. Do you want to master the skill or just become competent? Josh Kaufman, author of *The First 20 Hours: How to Learn Anything... Fast,* says it takes around 20 hours to gain a base level of competence.[118] This equates to deliberate practice of roughly 40 minutes each day, for a month. After that it becomes a harder process. His research shows that you reach a certain level of skill at around 20 hours before your rate of improvement declines and subsequent improvements take longer to accrue.

At the expert end of the scale, Dr K. Anders Ericsson, of Florida State University, found that it takes around ten years (or the often-quoted 10,000 hours) of practice to reach the top of ultra-competitive fields, such as professional golf, athletics, musical performance, or chess.[119] That equates to around four hours a day, five days a week. Most of us can breathe a sigh of relief, since being world-class in any given skill isn't normally the goal. In a work context we usually want to be competent rather than world-class, so the 10,000-hour rule doesn't apply, and we need to work from the base level of 20 hours.

MINDING YOUR BEHAVIOUR

> *When it comes to a behavioural shift, you have to take into account the amount of energy needed to fully embed a new behaviour or capability. Shifting one behaviour at a time is often the best way forward. It's important to keep a focus on the time needed to deliver lasting change, otherwise it should not be a surprise when the same initiatives come around year after year.*
> **Matt Burton - Head of Talent Development at DFS**

Changing behaviour is a little different. It can certainly be done a lot sooner than ten years, but perhaps not as quickly as you've been led to believe. There is a well-known maxim that it takes 21 days and/or 30 repetitions to create a habit. This comes from the 1950s, when plastic surgeon Dr Maxwell Maltz observed that those who underwent surgery with him took around 21 days to get used any cosmetic changes.[120] After that, they would not be taken by surprise when they caught their reflection in the mirror. Maltz subsequently penned *Psycho-Cybernetics*, an investigation into behavioural change, which subsequently sold tens of millions of copies. Regrettably, change is much more complex, he asserted.[121]

To embed a certain behaviour as second nature (i.e. a habit) takes much more effort. The latest behavioural science and psychology theory says it takes 200 repetitions of a behaviour to change it, with an average of 7–10 failures along the way, where you forget and go back to your old behaviour or habit. The important thing is to see these failures as part of the learning process. As long as the individual resets and remembers what went wrong, then each failure is just a step towards the 200 repetitions – and successful behavioural change.

How quickly can you expect behaviour change to happen, based on these findings? Phillippa Lally, a health psychology researcher at University College London found that, on average, it takes more than two months before a new behaviour becomes automatic (66 days to be precise).[122] Moreover, the time it takes to form a new habit can vary widely depending on the behaviour, the person, and the circumstances. In Lally's study, it took anywhere from 18 days to 254 days for someone to form a new habit.[123] The simple message is *changing behaviour takes time.* But if you align this principle with the practice of 'real-time learning' (see below), it will not only be time well spent, it will put you at the forefront of turning your business into a resilient, adaptable organisation, fit for 4IR.

REAL-TIME LEARNING

That core truth about behavioural change – that it takes time – is also a critical problem in 4IR. Time is the most precious commodity we have and when it comes to learning, there is never enough of it. That is why we need a new way of thinking about how we facilitate and deliver learning. That new way of thinking is real-time learning.

The focus of learning professionals for many years now has been to get learning out of the classroom and focused on 'micro learning' instead. This has seen practitioners embrace learning and development technology to deliver 'learning in the flow of work', a concept taken mainstream by Josh Bersin, and which we mentioned earlier.[124] At its heart though, this means offering learning opportunities in bite-sized formats, nudges that flow seamlessly into the daily work routine. This is absolutely the right approach to providing learning or knowledge that addresses individual needs. But we can do more. This does not often result in changing behaviours or embedding habits that deliver the productivity or innovations promised. We need 'in the flow of work 2.0'.

Ashridge Management College looked at the different modes of blended learning to see which was the most effective at changing behaviour and developing skills. Their rigorous methodology for measuring impact showed that, to change behaviour, the important thing is not the method of learning delivery you use. The answer lies in three key elements that must be included in any learning activity:

1. **An emotional experience** where participants undergo an intense learning point (i.e. something outside their normal

day-to-day experience and which they often struggle initially to make sense of).

2. **Support** to make sense of this learning point, helping them to reflect and to analyse it. This support can come from a peer, colleague, line manager or coach (thus enabling them to consciously understand what they've learnt).
3. **A plan** must then be implemented (in collaboration with the supporter above) to help the person transfer the key moment of learning into action over a period of time, facilitated by mutual support, encouragement, positive feedback and accountability.

Pioneers in learning and development realise self-directed learning isn't currently delivering the business value it promises and are using a new approach that helps embed learning into the organisation at a more fundamental level.

This real-time learning approach uses these three key elements above, with the purpose of baking in the core skills and behaviours, as well as the adaptability that will help your firm thrive in 4IR. Let us remind ourselves of the top five skills that will be required among employees to make any organisation thrive. They are:

1. Creativity and critical (connected) thinking.
2. Resilience and the ability to navigate through uncertainty.
3. Collaboration and building trust.
4. Complex problem solving and decision-making.
5. Influence and persuasion.

Without a new approach these will be difficult to embed. There needs to be a constant focus on them if they are to become part of the fabric of your organisation and that presents a barrier that can be difficult to cross.

But how can we do this when we have so little time in our day-to-day lives? The answer is to go with the flow. We already, or we will hopefully soon, have people getting together in more diverse and inclusive teams to solve complex business problems. Why not then develop skills for the future while solving real-time business problems?

To achieve this, you either need to be in the boardroom, the meeting room or on the shop floor and involved personally in the meeting wherever it takes place, or you need to establish a framework based on the six pillars of real-time learning which we will look at in 'X-Factor'. These require people to collaborate to solve a business problem and at the same time develop the five key skills for the future, as outlined above, or in fact, any other skills for that matter, which you see as critical for your people to develop. This process needs to capture learning needs and support skills development, whilst embedding leadership behaviours and habits that stick. You will be building the capability and belief of the individual, the team, and the organisation to be able to change, adapt and innovate, and then move beyond the hierarchy, the politics and the silo mentality.

This begins with identifying the performance improvement the business requires, the problem they want to solve, or the customer value they can add and deliberately building in the time and space for people to learn whilst in the flow of working on the strategic objective. Using the collective intelligence of people in the organisation to understand it and design the solution. At the same time developing their skills, habits, experiences and behaviours. There should be alignment between the goals of improving the performance of the organisation and the learning opportunity, and this clear connection between the learning experience and the business value should be made clear to everyone from the start. This is learning in the flow of work 2.0.

If you can do this then – whether you are in the room or not – you will be offering development in the moment when it is most effective. You will enable people to put a constant focus on fresh thinking, continuous learning and the skills that will future-proof your firm. Simultaneously, you will have overcome one of the top barriers to learning – time.

CAPEX – 'P' IS FOR PURPOSE

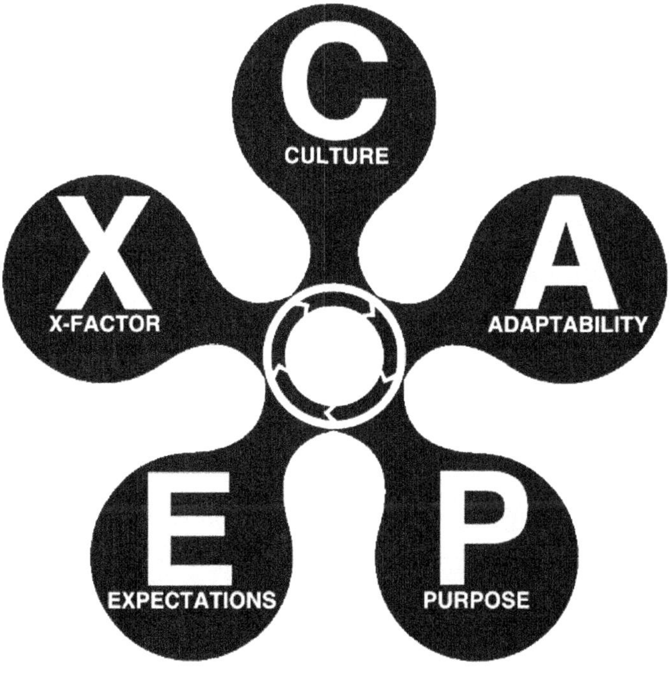

Defining, fostering and guarding organisational purpose has emerged as a key role of leaders in any forward-thinking organisation. A strong organisational purpose, clearly defined, and promoted inside and outside a business, will be a crucial differentiator of companies in the fourth industrial revolution.

A clear purpose will create long-term value by taking advantage of market opportunities, and it will address material risks. It will help build a company's reputation, affect its financial ratings, help it secure investment or access capital, boost recruitment and retention, and engage customers and suppliers.

No doubt you've seen companies waking up to this realisation with increasing frequency. Indeed, there is no shortage of visions and missions emblazoned across corporate websites to demonstrate that leaders are aware of the importance of organisational purpose. Increasingly, they can even tell you what it means.

This reflects the fact organisational purpose is already a key differentiator for companies. If we're looking for a nice, executive-friendly definition, we might call it:

> *An aspirational reason for being, which inspires and provides a call to action for an organisation and its partners and stakeholders, and provides benefit to local and global society.*[125]

You won't find many leaders these days who are brave enough to deny the importance of purpose, but getting some leaders to pay anything more than lip service to the notion is a different matter altogether.

These leaders see things like 'purpose', 'belief', or 'cause' as fuzzy, soft stuff, far removed from the cut and thrust of business. In this chapter we will give you the tools to show them how wrong they are.

Other leaders' hearts might be in the right place but they still struggle to align and embed purpose in day-to-day business. This is understandable: it can be awkward and can feel like it gets in the way of strategies, processes and structures that are firmly embedded and have, thus far, withstood the test of time.

Whatever stage you're at, purpose will become increasingly difficult to avoid. It will be a key driver of peak performance in 4IR. Driving organisational purpose should be – or quickly become – a fundamental consideration for commercial and strategic learning professionals. This is because purpose – and how it manifests itself – has become the key benchmark for companies. Often, this manifestation comes in the form of ESG, or Environment, Social, and Governance reporting. Other names often used interchangeably include Corporate Social Responsibility (CSR), Social Impact and Responsibility (SI&R), purpose-led reporting, sustainability reporting, and many more.

The ESG approach (or whatever you choose to call it) offers a wealth of opportunity for learning professionals because when it is done well, it links closely to business success. When done well, ESG reflects something known as 'double materiality', which covers:[126]

> **Financial materiality:** i.e. how ESG issues will impact a company's financial performance, and its impact on the companies ability to create long-term value.
> **Social materiality:** i.e. how a company's actions impact people and the Earth, which, dependent on the company's customers and employees, could have a significant impact on its brand and long-term value.

Let us look at the case of social materiality. There are whole industries – fossil fuels, for example – that are struggling to recruit the talent they need, as would-be employees can't get on board with their organisational purpose. On the flip-side, when it comes to financial materiality, there are large investment groups who will no longer deal with firms if they are deemed to operate an unsustainable environmental impact model. There are lots more examples below to whet the appetite of the hardiest business soul and help you build your case for the strategic application of organisational purpose.

The result is that purpose – that 'aspirational reason for being... that provides benefit to local and global society' – is no longer a fluffy, nice-to-have. It is a game-changer. And while the moral imperative ('doing the right thing') is always important, it is money that talks – and boy is it talking now.

You can help shape that conversation by mapping the learning needs of your business against its non-financial (i.e. purpose-driven) reporting. In doing so you are baking in long-term value for a whole host of stakeholders. If you want a better idea of what is covered by the ever-expanding ESG landscape (and hence what you can do to map your activities and drive that agenda forward), websites such as that of the ESG ratings agency MSCI offer a treasure trove of information.[127]

MAKING THE BUSINESS CASE

To cut a long story short, making a rock-solid business case that aligns learning with purpose – and makes it a strategic imperative – shouldn't be difficult. We'll look at exactly *where* you should focus in a moment.

A recent study in the *Harvard Business Review* looked at the C-Suite strategies of 28 companies in the United States, Europe, and India. What united these firms was that, for five years, they each grew by an average of 30% or over.[128] They equally all had executive teams who believed in purpose as a cornerstone of these results. They concurred that this aided them in:

- crafting a new business direction
- reconfiguring the organisation's values.[129]

This allowed them to maintain strong financial performance despite the obstacles placed in their way.[130] Focus on purpose helped the firms remain in touch with modern society. It helped them engage their stakeholders – whether they were staff, customers, partners or suppliers.[131] The question is why was this so effective?

Simon Sinek's 2009 TEDx Talk is one of the most popular of all time. It has over 50 million views. His message:

People don't buy what you do; people buy why you do it.[132]

This is because, as humans, our emotional motivation and connection is more important than our application of reason alone. If we have an emotional connection to the *purpose* of an organisation, then we tend to see that firm as unique and standing out from the crowd. That business can give us confidence of a better future, a sense of freedom, excitement and belonging. It can help make us feel secure and we better able to succeed.

For that reason, it is a much more powerful way of getting us to decide on who we wish to do business with – better than the product or service alone. Once we are sold on the *cause* of an idea, we'll go above and beyond to support it. We will support it with our money, our time, and, regarding social movements, even by some giving their lives. According to Sinek, if you want to inspire others, start by telling them why you do things, instead of what you do, and you'll see a massive change in engagement.

This is true of a wide range of stakeholders, but particularly pertinent for the staff that make any organisation succeed – the same people that learning professionals can have the greatest direct impact on. As such, getting colleagues to buy into your organisational purpose offers much more than just getting them on board. Organisational purpose creates a sense of meaning, inspiring employees and unlocking discretionary effort. If you can set that within a framework of shared values that is supported and led from the front by a united leadership team, you will see improvements in decision-making, innovation, productivity, and, ultimately, the bottom line. The business ROI is clear to see:

- The productivity levels of employees who are 'inspired' by purpose-led organisations, is almost triple that of 'disengaged' workers, per data from Bain & Company.[133] Moreover, those who are 'inspired' are more than twice as productive than even 'satisfied' staff.[134]
- Highly purposeful corporations have double the chance of realising better-than-average shareholder returns, according to Boston Consulting Group research.[135]

- Companies 'rated highly' for having a 'purposeful mission' have almost half the attrition rate of companies rated poorly on this dimension, according to the *2020 Global Talent Trends* report from LinkedIn.[136]

This all stems from staff having a sense of awareness and understanding that they, as individuals, are part of something that is not just bigger than themselves, but which shares their values.

Surely with all these benefits you would presume that firms are climbing over each other to demonstrate their organisational purpose? There certainly has been an increase over the last year, but research by professional services firm Grant Thornton found that only 50% of companies take steps to make apparent their social, value-driven purpose.[137] Those who can grasp the nettle of organisational purpose and make it work will find themselves with a clear competitive advantage.

CASE STUDY: UNILEVER AND PURPOSE-DRIVEN ROI

Unilever's stated purpose is 'to make sustainable living commonplace'.[138] This is driven by three core beliefs:[139]

- 'Brands with purpose grow.'
- 'Companies with purpose last.'
- 'People with purpose thrive.'

Employees at Unilever are supported to learn to identify and connect with their individual purpose in their passions through purpose workshops and are asked:

- What difference do you want to make in the world?
- What do you stand for?
- What ignites you?

This approach bakes purpose into the company culture. It is central to their strategy, not something they do as an add-on, and it is a core driver of the firm's success. There are, of course, other factors – political, economic, and so on – that play their part in the company's success. Unilever's sustainability policy (ranked highly in the Dow Jones Index[140]; agile working philosophy;[141] focus on diversity and inclusion (which has increased female managers from 38 to 50%[142]; and a data-led focus on the skills of the future[143], has driven global employee engagement to 88%.[144] The proportion of staff that say they are proud to work at Unilever is 93%, making it the number one large company in the world on this measure.

There are tangible benefits to this. Over the last decade Unilever has become the most sought-after employer in 54 out of 75 markets analysed.[145] This is the ability to attract and retain the best candidates and talent to its business through its company culture, leadership style, and employee engagement. The company has set itself the target of being number one in all markets.

The firm is, quite simply, getting access to the best people, getting better engagement from employees, and driving higher productivity. As such, it shouldn't come as a surprise that this purpose-led approach has coincided with a big rise in revenues and net profits. In the words of Alan Jope, Unilever CEO:

> *The key in this environment is to remain relevant to the consumers you serve. First, by earning trust by operating a responsible, multi-stakeholder business model. And second, by harnessing advances in science and technology – and especially digital – in ways that allow us to reach and delight consumers in new and ever more inventive ways.*[146]

Both these key tenets Mr Jope outlines as only possible with a strong organisational purpose driving them.

Unilever, FedEx, and MBDA exemplify the trend of aligning individual and organisational purposes. Alongside other world-class employers, FedEx and MBDA run programmes to help their employees discover their life purpose. MBDA, in particular, has been recognised for its efforts, being featured in prestigious lists such as The Sunday Times Best Places to Work, Glassdoor's Best Places to Work, and The Best Big Companies to Work For. Additionally, they stand out as one of the few UK companies to have achieved Gold in all Investors in People award categories

WHERE SHOULD YOU FOCUS? KEY STAKEHOLDERS IN ORGANISATIONAL PURPOSE

There are several groups that will benefit if you get your learning agenda properly aligned with organisational purpose. The reason they will benefit is because the business itself is benefitting and as such, you will see the returns generated by investing in learning.

INVESTORS

Perhaps here, more than anywhere else, the alignment of purpose and business ROI can be most clearly shown. Throughout history investors have often been part of the problem, not the solution, when it comes to organisations turning their eyes towards the notion of a higher purpose than profits at any cost. Companies have a legal duty to do the best by their investors – their owners – that they can. This has, in the past, translated into maximising profits at the expense of such trifling matters as the health of the planet. This cannot – and will not – go on.

The proof that this is the case is growing every day. Take Unilever's 28 Sustainable Living Brands, which grew 69% quicker than the rest of their business in 2018.[147] They were also responsible for 75% of Unilever's overall growth.[148] Figures like that make investors sit up and listen. This clearly demonstrates that genuine purpose done right leads to increased profits, as Bill Theofilou of Accenture Strategy noted in an interview with *Forbes*.[149]

Then there is BlackRock. Whatever their motive for the move, it was an extraordinary moment in 2020 when the fund management giant pledged to vote against directors of companies that wouldn't take enough action on climate change. BlackRock boss Larry Fink put listed companies on note that this could happen in his annual letter to chief executives.[150] Again, there was nothing fluffy here, it was about solid, long-term growth. Mr Fink focused on the 'significant and lasting impact [climate change] will have economic growth and prosperity'.[151] In big, bold letters he stated: 'Climate Risk Is Investment Risk'.[152]

Fink's firm is joined by others, including Standard Chartered, who now refuse to finance new coal power stations[153] and many other sorts of coal initiatives and activities.[154] More investors will take a stand as 4IR progresses. Latterly, Oxford and Harvard researchers have demonstrated that 82.1% of 'mainstream investors' ponder ESG data – that is, the environmental, social and governance factors we mentioned earlier – in considering investment opportunities.[155]

The impact of this is being felt. Professional Services firm KPMG stated that more than three in four of the CEOs it surveyed thought that their company's adaptation to the green economy would dictate its future growth prospects.[156] This shift was couched in terms of the environment and benefitting society, but this was accompanied by a more telling narrative around 'unlock[ing] growth' through creating new market opportunities and making operations more efficient.[157] Two years prior, in the same survey, climate change didn't even make it into the list of the CEOs' top five risks.[158] Their views have now clearly changed.

EMPLOYEES

In the battle for talent that the Fourth Industrial Revolution will usher in, there is a clear choice to make about your organisation's place and purpose in a global community. If you want to recruit and retain the best employees from the widest possible pool then you must pay attention to purpose. We're not just talking about looking after their individual needs, but addressing a much bigger picture.

In a recent survey by Deloitte, Millennial workers (those born between 1981 and 1996)[159] were asked what the primary purpose of business should be. 'Improv[ing] society' beat 'Generat[ing] profit' by a margin of 4 percentage points.[160] The Edelman Trust Barometer offers a wider perspective but a similar result. It found that 66% of people want CEOs to 'take the lead' in acting on societal issues, instead of looking to the government.[161] A full 86% of survey respondents want CEOs 'to publicly speak out' more on issues ranging from controversial political and social issues to workplace automation, and local problems.[162]

These are the new rules in the battle for talent and your firm will find it increasingly difficult to win if you don't recognise and adapt to them.

CUSTOMERS

People no longer believe governments are the answer to the world's most challenging issues. In one study, almost nine out of ten (88%) British and American consumers wanted companies 'to [assist them in] improv[ing] their environmental and social footprint'.[163]

We live in a febrile environment where societal issues can surface, almost from nowhere, and challenge an organisation. Take the BBC's *Blue Planet II*, which was widely credited with sparking a full-blown 'war on plastic'.[164] In its annual food and drink survey, UK supermarket Waitrose reported that 88% of respondents who saw the episode in question had changed their behaviour as a consequence.[165] Waitrose subsequently received eight times more plastic-related enquiries from consumers.[166]

From what we already know about the public's priorities, it is a safe bet that the implication for most people is that because business can make a difference, it should. If an organisation cannot align itself with a higher purpose than its own interests, the battle for talent and customers might be lost – regardless of their lightning fast 4IR technologies.

HOW TO MAKE PURPOSE TAKE HOLD

We hope the business case for focusing on organisational purpose is now clear, as are some of the areas that might help you shape your approach to the wider subject. Now let us now look at how you can embed and leverage purpose at different levels within your business.

INDIVIDUAL PURPOSE

In the corporate world, purpose is often framed by, and enshrined in, big, world-changing concepts. There is often a huge gap between the purpose and blueprint created by senior leaders and its relevance and meaning to colleagues on the front line. It is crucial to make sure that, whatever the drivers of your organisational purpose, they are aligned to the individual purposes of the people who actually make up that organisation.

That might sound like a monstrous task. How can you possibly serve the purpose of every individual? Well, it is easier than you might think, particularly if you understand what lies at the root of individual purpose and how we are bound together by it.

Firstly, we need to accept that a need for purpose is a fundamental human need that is being increasingly exacerbated by the social and technological advances of 4IR. But, while the need and the opportunity for the expression of individual purpose is growing, it is not new.

Man's Search For Meaning, by Victor E Frankl, is a ground-breaking book on individual purpose.[167] It tells of the horrifying experiences of holocaust survivors in Nazi concentration camps and how Frankl became convinced that what helped him and others survive was the search for meaning in their lives. He noticed that it was the men who comforted others and who gave away their last piece of bread who survived the longest. It was purpose that allowed people to transcend their suffering and find significance in what they were doing, and keep going. Whilst this is an extreme example, it shows the amazing things individuals can do and the positive decisions they make when they have a sense of purpose. The same mindset is what you are nurturing to navigate the uncertainty and challenges faced in the new world of work.

This sense of individual purpose is often intuitive and formed early in life, but that doesn't mean people won't have to search hard for it. In some Native American cultures, it is believed that each person is born to fulfil a purpose in the world but that they must discover it. As children, we start to detect our purpose around seven or eight years old as our strengths and passions start to become clear. In our teens we can start to reflect on our purpose. Unfortunately, school systems and society all-too-often distract us from that journey of discovery, or encourage us to bury our feelings deep if they don't match expectations.

In Japan, millions of people look to ikigai. According to Héctor García, co-author of *Ikigai: The Japanese Secret to a Long and Happy Life,* this is 'the intersection of what you are good at and what you love doing'. What follows is a summary of the ideas contained in his book. [168]

He adds:

> *Just as humans have lusted after objects and money since the dawn of time, other humans have felt dissatisfaction at the relentless pursuit of money and fame and have instead focused on something bigger than their own material wealth. This has over the years been described using many different words and practices, but always hearkening back to the central core of meaningfulness in life.*

Ikigai has four core elements:

1. Your passion – what you love.
2. Your purpose or mission – what the world needs.
3. Your vocation – what you are good at.
4. Your profession – what you can get paid for.

But we can go even deeper than this. We can strip everything away and examine the common human drivers we all share and which lie at the heart of successfully engaging organisational purpose. It is these drivers that will enable you to connect the individuals in your organisation, engaging them with the company's wider mission.

These underlying factors have always been with us, but the shape and structure of society and work have often enabled employers to ignore them in the past. Workers were there to do what they were told to do and they could like it or lump it. However, changing demographics, technologies and social movements have changed the workplace in a way that means they can be ignored no longer. Instead they should be embraced to shape your organisational purpose and drive business success.

Building on the works of David Rock in neuroscience[169] and Tony Robbins in business and personal development,[170] We have created a list of eight core human needs which learning professionals need to be mindful of when driving internal engagement with purpose. Keeping these needs in mind will give you a solid bedrock as you support colleagues in their business-critical conversations and decisions, as you help develop your organisation's narrative, culture and strategy.

1. CERTAINTY

We have a deep need for certainty in life. We crave stability in our relationships, health, and financial wellbeing. We seek safety, security, comfort, order, predictability, control and consistency. We get this from clarity of expectations, and an alignment of our purpose and values, as much as we get it from financial security and other more obvious drivers.

2. SIGNIFICANCE

We need to feel that we are important to other people; that we have status and reputation. We want to avoid being invisible and irrelevant. We need to feel understood and special; we need to have pride, feel needed, and have a sense of importance and worth.

3. CONNECTION

Beyond having significance to others, we also have a deep need to be connected and loved for who we are. We do not want to be left disconnected, alone, and unappreciated. We are social animals, and we naturally form social groups, tribes and build relationships. These groups build mutual trust and form a barrier against the unknown. We need love, communication, empathy, approval and to feel connected to others. Belonging is an unspoken benefit of working in a team, like being part of a family or group of friends.

4. VARIETY

Human beings need surprises and adventure in life. We do not want to be bored by experiencing the same predictable things every single day. We need challenges, excitement, difference, adventure and change.

5. AUTONOMY

Autonomy gives a person a sense of control over what they do. Without autonomy we can feel under threat and suffer stress as a result. We need to feel we have options, a voice, and that we can make our own decisions. We want to feel that we are empowered and can influence others. Fundamentally, we want to think we are free.

6. CONTRIBUTION

We have an intense need to contribute to something greater than ourselves. We need to share what we have with others to get the most fulfilment out of life possible. Our talents and belongings do little to help us if we keep them just to ourselves. It is a human need to give, protect and serve others.

7. GROWTH

We need to feel like we are always growing and making progress. We do not want to feel like we are standing still, stagnating or, worse still, becoming obsolete (particularly when we are increasingly competing with both people and machines in 4IR). We need continuous emotional, intellectual and spiritual development. Continuous learning is a hallmark of high-performing individuals and high-performing teams.

8. FAIRNESS

We need transparency and candour in our dealings with others. Collaboration requires the different parties to feel what is being done is right and fair. If a person thinks something is unfair, their brain automatically goes into defence mode – fight, flight, or freeze. We need straight-forward, simple, honest and sometimes courageous conversations. We need balance (give and take), openness and fair treatment. It is hardly surprising that even the youngest children are so quick (and loud!) in their protests that 'IT'S NOT FAIR!' when they perceive another getting preferential treatment.

These needs go to the heart of happiness, trust, and wellbeing – and ultimately a sense of purpose. When our needs are not being met, we are likely to perform worse than we otherwise might. At work, people often indicate which of their needs are not being met when they complain about things. For example, they might say, 'My boss is micromanaging me', when the unmet needs are autonomy and freedom. Or they may say, 'Our senior management team is being unclear about the impact of AI on our working practices,' when the unmet needs are certainty and security. These fundamental human drivers may be ancient, but they are connected to, and influenced by, current macro trends. As such we need to be able to understand them in the context of these trends.

Let us take another example – and another macro trend that we have already touched on: flexible working and the gig economy. As technology advances it seems likely this will only grow. If that's the case, it seems logical that the value people put on their experiences and their voice being heard will grow. In turn it follows that other workplace factors that previously were important – like having the appropriate job title – will recede as they will not confer the right to having a voice in the way they once did.

These examples might sound like small things when taken in isolation. But if, for example, your analysis of such factors allows the firm to improve its offer to current and would-be employees, then you will quickly see returns in terms of lower turnover, quicker times to hire, and so on.

In her book *Quiet: The Power of Introverts in a World That Can't Stop Talking*, Susan Cain points out that around a third to a half of the working population are introverts.[171] They need time and space to think and to be creative, to be productive and to be happy. The world of back-to-back meetings and open-plan offices is, Cain says, designed for extroverts.[172] Conversely, being able to work from home more often will satisfy an introvert's need both for autonomy and for fairness. But as soon as you've got your head round this, the question arises about how you will address the impact on the human need for connection. For some, the experience of flexible working could be described as heaven, while others will suffer from feeling isolated and out of touch.

The desire for flexibility is a driving force in the hybrid world of work and this puts new demands on companies and their leaders. But it will be your understanding of human drivers in this – or any other – context, and the steps you take to evolve your organisation culture, that could be the key to getting greater engagement and higher productivity from a large swathe of your colleagues.

Like a dial on a radio, the weight that should to be put on the different human needs can be turned up and down in your organisations as you develop the vision and mission – and hence, purpose – that will enable you to deliver on your business goals. But they all need to be turned on to some extent. They need to be in balance for people to truly engage with your company and its purpose, and drive the business results we are looking for.

Business cultures which tap into all eight human needs create the type of positive workplaces people want to work in. These will be workplaces where colleagues are engaged and want to go the extra mile. Your holistic approach to engaging with their needs on a fundamental level will pay dividends. In this new era we can't expect people to leave part of themselves at the door if we want them to succeed at what they are doing. They need to be encouraged to be authentic and bring their whole self to work. This will not only make them happier, but will all mean they are more connected and trusted by their colleagues. You can facilitate all of this. As Microsoft CEO Staya Nadella wrote in a letter to employees:

> *It is in times of great disruption and uncertainty that our ability to stay grounded in our sense of purpose and remain true to our identity is of the utmost importance.*[173]

It is also important to understand the subtle difference between human needs and values. These concepts are deeply interconnected and both reflect the things we care about. The difference is human needs are a part of us all – they are common to everyone and the bedrock of what it means to be human. Our values, on the other hand, express our personal interpretation of those needs. They are highly personal, profoundly held and deeply treasured. Both needs and values are socially driven and moulded. They affect our thoughts and feelings. They guide our decisions and our behaviour. They define our character. They are the things that make us jump out of bed in the morning. If our values are not being met, this can create a sense of discontent, a lack of energy or motivation, and lead to stress and conflict.

Of course, organisations can't be expected to cater of every value that each employee holds dear. But there is a way to help ensure the best possible fit and that is by working to align individual and organisational core values. If you can't do that for any given person, there is a good chance that employee is in the wrong job.

What, then, defines an organisation's values? Simply put, organisational values reflect the collective understanding of what is important to the organisation. They shape the culture, identity, beliefs, and the philosophy of the business. They define how, day-by-day, the company will act. As such, they sit at the heart of its purpose.

Values make it clear to potential customers, employees, and partners what the company stands for, how it will behave, and what it expects from its stakeholders (e.g. employees, suppliers, partners, etc). When organisational values are lived day-to-day and are communicated throughout the business, decision-making becomes quicker and easier. Making value-based decisions, linked to organisational purpose, gives us clarity and allows us to focus on what is important.

All this will feed individual purpose and ensure alignment at an organisational level. From here, the benefits will quickly accumulate. Research by Amy Wrzesniewski and her academic colleagues found people with meaning and purpose not only find their work more rewarding,[174] but work harder and longer. As a result, she concluded, these were also the people more likely to be successful. She also found that, fundamentally, it didn't matter what type of job one has, it has as much to do with mindset as it has with the actual work being done.

A team of researchers, including Anthony Burrow, a developmental psychologist and director of the Purpose and Identity Processes Laboratory at Cornell University, found that purpose helps us combat everyday stressors and process our emotions.[175] This, in turn, helps improve their wellbeing, health and performance.[176] Another study Burrow was involved in showed that participants with purpose 'earned on average $2,578 more a year and had a net worth $14,680 greater than those [without]'.[177]

As a learning professional it will be up to you to make sure people have the support they need and are encouraged to connect with their individual purpose, and bring their whole selves to work. You need to foster an environment where it is safe for people to speak up, to be themselves, and to follow their passions. This comes with the obvious caveat that these elements must exist within the framework of your organisational purpose. If individual purpose and organisational purpose cannot co-exist, it might be time for those people to be 'happy elsewhere' and look to others organisations for professional fulfilment.

Before we move on we'll leave you with some powerful words of currently unknown provenance that nevertheless sum up the quest for individual purpose so well:

> *The two most important days in your life are the day you are born and the day you find out why.*[178]

TEAM PURPOSE

Nurturing purpose amongst teams is subtly different from that of individual purpose and your wider organisational purpose. Team purpose is often the connector bringing individual purpose closer to organisational purpose. In this way colleagues move from being cogs in a machine to essential elements of a living, breathing organism. Of course, some organisations have such a powerful sense of purpose attached to them that the sense of belonging to a higher purpose is enough for individual people. That said, most firms are not so well focused.

Team purpose gives people a sense of identity and belonging; of a connection to the group of people they work with every day. In its own way, team purpose brings organisational purpose to life by helping people understand their own importance and distinct contribution to the larger vision. It is an old military trope that soldiers might not be interested in – or even understand – the cause they are fighting for, but will be willing to fight and die for the person standing next to them. This is an extreme example of how teams can channel individual purpose to enable people to serve something bigger than themselves.

Mark Truelson, building on the work of Simon Sinek,[179] encourages us to think of an organisation like a tree, where the roots and trunk represent its origin and foundation, while the branches are divisions and departments of that business. On those branches sit nests, each of which represents a subculture or team. Within each nest is a family of birds who belong together.[180]

In this analogy, it is individual purpose that drives us to find the correct tree and the right nest. The goal of an organisation then is to know what purpose it needs to have to offer an attractive home to the birds it needs to complement its ecosystem. The goal for each team within the company is to make sure those birds are in the right nests; birds that will work together effectively to ultimately contribute to the organisation's higher purpose and cause.

This raises an interesting conundrum: what if the bird is in the right tree and on the right branch, but in the wrong nest? Well then, you've got problems. This can hurt the performance, morale and self-confidence of both the individual and the wider team. Learning professionals can act as important enablers here; ensuring peoples' talents are effectively leveraged. The quickest solution to this problem is to support team leaders in establishing a sense of 'Why?' in their team. What is it they are there to do? Why does it matter? What skills are needed to fulfil the 'Why'? Helping align teams behind their leaders in this way can bring all sorts of benefits: raised morale, higher productivity, better retention rates… the list goes on.

High-performing sports teams offer useful insights into creating common purpose within a team. The most successful can maintain their dominance year after year, even as talented individuals on the team come and go. The authors of *Peak Performance: Business Lessons from the World's Top Sports Organisations* conclude that the key lesson is individual values and purpose must be aligned to organisation values and purpose.[181] As such, the team exists to reconcile these two levels of purpose.

Phil Jackson, former coach to Michael Jordan and the world-beating Chicago Bulls basketball team, also spoke to this sense of shared purpose when he said:

> *The most effective way to forge a winning team is to call on the players' need to connect to something larger than themselves. Even for those who don't consider themselves 'spiritual' in a conventional sense, creating a successful team – whether it's an NBA champion or a record-setting sales force – is essentially a spiritual act. It requires the individuals involved to surrender their self-interest for the greater good so that the whole adds up to more than the sum of its parts.*[182]

This 'spiritual' approach and the success it brings can be found wherever firms have successfully engaged employees and their passions with a powerful organisational purpose, and then channelled the resulting talent and energy through purpose-driven teams. This is true – and demonstrable – whether you look at Tesla working to transition the world to sustainable transport,[183] Innocent Drinks' purpose,[184] which one Prezi user sums up as being, 'to make food good',[185] or Google's aim to empower people with information.[186]

SOCIAL PURPOSE

More than ever, people across the world – driven by the scenes they see and stories they read on their various connected devices – understand that the air that we breathe is the air that everyone breathes; that the water we drink, is the water that everyone drinks. They see how someone putting carbon into the air or plastic into the sea – whether nearby or on the other side of the planet – affects them, their families and their friends. We need to work ever more closely together to address the challenges of an integrated world. And if this is the case in the 'real world', it is certainly the case for organisations.

Organisations are no longer seen as isolated entities that should focus on serving their shareholders (whatever that might mean for their employees, customers, and other stakeholders). Today there is a rapidly growing belief that businesses must have a meaningful impact on society – and *be seen* to be having a meaningful impact – as well as doing right by the communities they serve, and by the planet.

As we've already seen, social purpose – often encapsulated under the moniker of 'sustainability' – has become business-critical, driven by a heady cocktail of investor pressure, consumer attitudes, employee activism, regulation, politics, competitive advantage and moral imperative. Staff, potential employees, suppliers, partners, customers, and others, often won't accept anything less. Unsurprisingly, a recent Deloitte and Forbes Insights global survey of CEOs found that their top metric for assessing performance was 'societal impact'.[187] The examples listed for this category were, unsurprisingly, 'diversity', 'inequality' and 'environment'.[188]

Nevertheless, 'social purpose' is a broad topic. The question of where to start is a tough one. We would suggest the UN Global Compact, 'the world's largest corporate sustainability initiative'.[189] It advances 'business as a force for good', bringing corporations together that are working for an improved future – or a future at all, for that matter.[190] Its core principles cover four areas that can act as signposts for advancing your organisational purpose:[191]

- human rights
- labour
- environment
- anti-corruption.

There is a lot of detail here that can help you shape your framework and a lot of opportunity for you to do the right thing, in both social and financial terms. And while progress is taking place, Lise Kingo, CEO & Executive Director of the UN Global Compact, says:

> *There are huge gaps, particularly on climate change and inequality – for women, young people and for workers in the global supply chain. This is where business can make a huge difference.*[192]

This is your opportunity to be part of the solution and to differentiate your business at the same time (and reap the rewards for it).

Learning professionals have a great chance to start the conversations, analyse the place and role of their organisation in society, and create rigorous goals and outcomes to drive a tangible sense of purpose. Each individual business will have different drivers that correspond with its vision and mission, as well as its operational circumstances. Our experience tell us we will see a greater number of workshops to support staff in discovering their individual life purpose and passions, as well as how they can fulfil those both at work and outside it. We will see pioneers working with teams to align the different levels of purpose (organisational, team, individual and social), creating a widespread uplift in the perception of meaning in people's lives, in turn increasing engagement and connection to the business. We will see greater matching of individual passions and career aspirations with strategic organisational goals.

We will also see and benefit from a much wider development in connected thinking, ensuring purpose is brought into business meetings and decisions. This will lead to our organisational skills and capabilities being leveraged in ways we might never have thought of to serve our purpose – ensuring our businesses avoid stagnation and remain relevant.

The questions for learning professionals come thick and fast… How can we adapt our operation to better serve our organisational purpose? How can we change the way people work to suit both them and our business better? Can we facilitate a more flexible workplace, whilst ensuring an equitable experience for every employee? What can we do better or differently, in terms of how we interact with employees, customers, suppliers and partners?

MAKE PURPOSE HAPPEN

If you can bring learning to the forefront of the embedding of multiple layers of purpose within your business you will see extraordinary results. As we have seen, organisational cultures that are purpose- and values-driven double, or even triple, productivity, reduce attrition rates, make more profit, and are twice as likely to deliver shareholder returns. This is being driven by employees, the media, governments, customers, suppliers and now investors, who are demanding that firms be 'world citizens' run on a sustainable agenda.

Once upon a time this approach would have horrified many a business leader. But the growing environmental crisis, ever-scarcer resources and democratised workplaces, coupled with opportunity 4IR technology offers to deliver business in a way that would have been unthinkable just a few years ago, has changed all that. The circle is a virtuous one. It delivers on a planet-wide drive for good corporate citizenship, but also on an ever-growing human need for personal certainty and significance, balanced with the desire to be part of something bigger than oneself. That desire is driven by a profound need to be play a role in something that matters; to spend one's days in a place where you can find happiness and approval, openness and fairness, as well as a connection with others; somewhere you can learn and grow and contribute as you develop emotionally, intellectually and spiritually. In short, somewhere you can find purpose.

CAPEX – 'E' IS FOR EXPECTATIONS

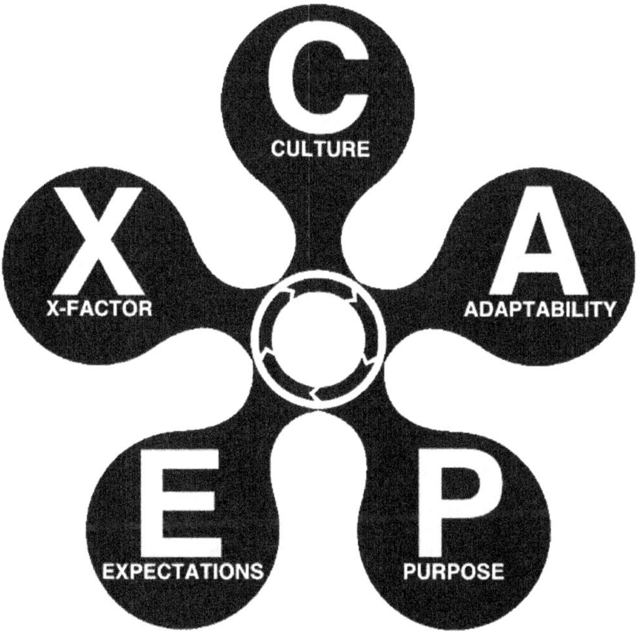

For centuries, Europeans believed all swans were white. This was an accepted truth. When anyone spoke about or saw a swan, they were quite certain that it would be white.[193] Although they was almost certainly an earlier sighting,[194] one often repeated story is that a group of Dutch explorers captained by Willem de Vlamingh were the first Europeans to see black swans in 1697 on an expedition to Australia.[195] Regardless of the true order of events, it must have seemed impossible to whoever first spotted them, and yet there they were. For this reason, Nassim Nicholas Taleb calls events like this, which seem impossible but evidently aren't, 'Black Swans'.[196] He notes that, in hindsight – but unfortunately not foresight – they are actually very much predictable.[197]

The Fourth Industrial Revolution (4IR) will be a time of Black Swans when it comes to people's changing expectations of their workplaces. Some of these expectations will completely change how some parts of the workplace are run, while others will augment aspects that we are familiar with – the incumbent white swans, if you will.

A lot of people are already struggling with how these expectations are changing – and they ain't seen nothing yet. These difficulties are hardly surprising given that workplaces were, for many, many years, governed by the same inalienable, ingrained truths: men ruled the roost; your boss would be older than you; you worked in one place and lived in another; work and play were separate things; you would retire at a set age… the examples go on and on. Once upon a time this was completely acceptable from a business perspective. It might have been unfair, inconvenient, or unproductive, but it was the status quo. It was expected. It was OK.

It is not OK any more.

Expectations of what a workplace should be are changing rapidly and it is crucial learning professionals understand the new dynamics that are shaping them so businesses can benefit from the changes, rather than fighting a losing battle against them.

Once you understand what those expectations are, you will need to create experiences that meet and fulfil them. Or to put it another way: new expectations demand new experiences; experiences that will be personalised and inclusive; experiences that will give employees moments that *matter*, be it to an individual or a group. And when it comes to creating these experiences, you'll need to be laser focused on alignment with the outside world. They will need to be honest and authentic. They will need to align the employee experience with the customer experience and a host of other workplace stakeholders.

These experiences cannot stand alone either; they will exist as part of a work lifecycle that has job candidates at one end of the journey and alumni at the other. Each group will be one vertical in a holistic people experience that offers critical, career-defining learning opportunities, enabling them to develop the skills they need to solve problems and advance the business.

HOW EXPECTATIONS OF THE WORKPLACE ARE CHANGING

The future remains difficult to predict, but we can isolate a few macro trends that will almost certainly shape how companies look and feel, as well as how they will be expected to treat their people. Every progressive organisation will need to consider these trends – on top of all the other day-to-day, established expectations a workforce has – if they want to create workplaces that the most talented people want to join and stay in.

The learning profession will be crucial in engaging with, and facilitating, these trends, which include:

- Offering staff consumer-like experiences.
- Being inclusive and diverse.
- Nurturing a global, multi-generational workplace.

EXPECTATION ONE: CONSUMER-LIKE EXPERIENCES

The demands for modern people and culture strategies, as well as learning experiences, can only be understood when put in the context of wider consumer expectations. The line between home and work life is becoming increasingly blurred and employees are having their workplace expectations shaped increasingly by their experiences as consumers.

As 4IR advances, employees and other business stakeholders will become less willing to see a distinction between their highly-personalised and user-friendly daily life, and what their work life has to offer. The wider the gap between them, the lower engagement you will get. This will impact how effectively you can deliver everything from wide-ranging cultural programmes, to individual learning. Employees now expect products and services – including those delivered by the learning function – to be delivered with the:

- speed of Google
- community of Airbnb
- design of Apple
- responsiveness of Uber
- convenience of Amazon
- entertainment factor of Red Bull.

It is principles like these that will underlie the kind of intuitive and empathetic design thinking that will drive any successful 4IR workplace experience. So, when thinking about our learning strategies, services and products, we need to ask whether they are being delivered in a way that:

- offers immediate access to knowledge (i.e. if a colleague needs something the solution needs to be at their fingertips)
- helps create or bolster a feeling of community
- is easy to use (with the technology delivering seamlessly in the background)
- is responsive to the target individual's personal needs
- is convenient and delivered within the natural flow of their work
- is easily assessable at the time and in the place they want to learn.

That might seem like a challenging checklist, but why should we expect employees to put up with an experience in the workplace that would be considered substandard outside of it?

So, yes, learning has quite the task to get up-to-date with consumer expectations, but it is also important you aren't always chasing the agenda when you have the opportunity to shape it. To do this, you need to look in places you might not expect for inspiration. As Steve Jobs once famously said:

> *Our job is to figure out what they're going to want before they do… People don't know what they want until you show it to them. That's why I never rely on market research. Our task is to read things that are not yet on the page.*[198]

In the book *Trend-driven Innovation* the authors challenge us to answer the question that naturally follows Mr Jobs' assertion: 'How do you understand what your customers are going to want *next*?'[199] According to Henry Mason, one of the book's four co-authors, the key to anticipating what people will want next is to stop looking at your customers or industry rivals and start looking at innovative businesses that are setting customer expectations, in terms of what is possible, desirable or simply 'normal'. The insights you can draw from them are what will help you anticipate what your customers will want and what your rivals will do next.

The simple truth is that customers' future needs and wants are shaped by what's delighting them right now. One archetypal example of this is consumers flocking to Apple devices because of the seamlessness user experience. We live in a convenient, transparent, on-demand society. This has impacted everyone's expectations. Before Uber, no one gave a second thought to waiting 15 or 20 minutes for a taxi. Children in the '80s gave no thought to early computer games taking 20 minutes to load. Which gamer would accept that now? If you look to services in the wider world and take time to understand what drives their use and peoples' enjoyment of them, you can then benchmark your offerings against them. These services are joined up, connected and smart. Often, entirely different services work seamlessly together across hardware and software. They are an integrated feature of our daily lives. These indicators are key facets of 4IR and should be the benchmark for organisations wishing to effectively engage with their employees. Anything less and you will fall into the trap of poor service that is so often the perceived hallmark of learning and development functions.

Without the addition of 4IR tech none of this would be possible, obviously. But that's the whole point. It is 4IR tech that is shaping the rest of the world and we must let it shape ours. That tech might well take us into the realms of virtual reality learning, avatar-based training simulations, gamification and who knows where else.

What we mustn't forget in this tech whirlwind is *why* tech is so important. That reason is not new, in fact it is as old as time. It is as old as the first cave person sitting down to take notes on the making of the latest tech called the wheel. The reason we love the tech is because it can make learning engaging; it can make it fun. When that is the case, 'learning is a drug' according to Ralph Koster, the best-selling author of *A Theory of Fun for Game Design*.[200] Koster spent a lot of time looking at why gamers would spend days, months and even years playing. Hour after hour they went on with nothing to motivate them other than learning and getting better.[201] Therein lay the key: they were striving to learn in an engaging, accessible way. Learning was their drug. But Koster also warned the enjoyment and fulfilment they were getting could quickly be killed if boredom set in. Whether you are a keen gamer or find the whole phenomenon baffling, there is an inescapable lesson we can all draw from this.

CASE STUDY: MEETING EXPECTATIONS AT SANTANDER BANK

Earlier we met Robert Ashcroft, Head of Capability at Santander bank. We looked at how he had restructured his team and built products that would give them the ability to deliver real time learning (and we will look at Robert's real-time learning strategy in depth later).

One thing that enabled Santander's Capability team to successfully deliver this agenda was their excellent understanding of their internal clients' expectations and – crucially – putting those expectations in the context of their experience as 21st Century consumers.

> *Our major step-change came when we stopped measuring ourselves against other learning practitioners and started measuring ourselves against other consumer-grade services and products,' says Robert. 'When you start looking outwardly and start comparing L&D to what we would do in normal life, that is where you shift your thinking and how you start to stride towards a really great, engaging experience.*

In Robert's eyes this meant setting the bar very high indeed.

> *We wanted to deliver the kind of quality and fidelity of experience that was as close as possible to what you got outside of work,' he says. 'Employees – our customers – needed to be talking about our products in the same way they talked about their consumer grade products. How they scrutinise Netflix should be the same as how they scrutinise our experience platform.*

To do that the team had to accept that a traditional approach to instructional design wasn't good enough; what they needed were people who understood storytelling.

For Santander, this started with high-quality film content that really drove emotion and connectivity. This was crucial to the team's three-stage approach to learning: 'experience, reflection, action'.

> *I wanted to watch a piece of film that would enable me – and hence our customers – to have an emotional connection with that experience and then go through my reflection and take a course of action,' Robert says. 'I want the kind of compelling video that charities use to help people part with their money; something that makes me say "I'm going to change my ways".*

This commitment to quality was the same across all the team's output, whatever the medium.

> *If someone goes to one of our in-person events, that needs to be as powerful as going to one of the best rock concerts in your life; it need to be something you'll tell your mates about. When it came to the written word, we looked really closely at why some magazines and articles get read, or blogs visited, more than others; what is it about the design and language that's used that does that? In the end it's all about good strong storytelling.*

Using this approach, the uptake of discretionary learning products rocketed at Santander. But Robert was keen to test his team's output with the best outside the organisation too.

> *We don't need to chasing learning awards, we need to be judged by the same awarding panels as those that judge consumer panels.*

Among the accolades that followed were a Cannes Corporate film award for Santander's 'Losing Mr Renton' series about vulnerable customers, which used real recordings of customer calls. Another Cannes Corporate award followed the next year, as have awards from EVLDN Clarion for 'excellence in cause-driven corporate film, live events and experiences', and others.

For Robert, key to getting this right is to understand what his customers want and expect. Whenever his team designs a new learning product they engage the customer throughout, constantly checking and testing what they are doing is going to land well with the audience.

> *This process is so important. The difference between getting this right or wrong is why some drama series run for two seasons and some run for seven… And why some run for ten and should have only run for seven!*

EXPECTATION TWO: INCLUSION AND DIVERSITY

Inclusion and diversity might appear a strange inclusion in a book on a new – and almost futuristic – era. The idea has been pushed into the mainstream for a number of years. The difference now is when we talk about business inclusivity and diversity, we do so in its widest sense. Categories like gender, age and ethnicity are key, but we must also consider other differentiators like cultural and social backgrounds, abilities, personalities, strengths, even thinking styles. The latter categories – often lumped together under the title of neurodiversity – arise from 'the variation and differences in [brain] structure and function'.[202] It is when we recognise and value difference in its broadest sense that we start realising the greatest benefits.

Yet many businesses are still a long way off even considering such nuanced approaches to inclusion and diversity. Big, obvious solutions still elude them.

Many approach this area from a predominantly risk-based perspective, asking questions such as, 'how can we make sure we don't appear unwilling to accommodate someone's disability?' rather than taking a more proactive approach which is focused on opportunity, asking alternative questions such as: 'how can we create an equitable experience for every employee?' or 'how can we develop an inclusive culture that impacts every stage of the employee life cycle in order to generate ethical and commercial return on investment?'. The latter style encourages inclusive practice rather than scrambling for compliance and avoiding negative publicity.

Take the example of disability. Whether through prejudice, unwillingness, or practical difficulties, there are still many firms that shy away from hiring people with disabilities. Yet, the World Health Organisation and World Bank estimate that there are a billion people in the world currently living with a disability. At the time they made this calculation, that constituted about 15% of the global population, or one in seven of us.[203] Ignoring the vast pool of talent in this group is to make solving the complex problems we face – and will face in ever greater numbers – much more difficult.

Jay Muthu, Director – Organisational and People Capability at Entain Group says:

> *Everyone in the corporate world will organise webinars on disability inclusion on International Day of Persons with Disabilities and then get on with their life until next year; can we normalise disability and take action to address the disability employment gap?*

This example, and others like it, offer big and easy wins for firms. Once they've done that then they can start on our 4IR definition of inclusion and diversity.

We must also be careful to differentiate diversity from inclusion. As Verna Myers puts it: 'Diversity is being invited to the party; inclusion is being asked to dance'.

If we want to get the best out of people, we need to focus, as best we can, on each individual's experience within the workplace and in wider society, and the extent to which they feel they belong, are valued and included. Steps you can take to do this include greater local and distributed decision-making (more on that shortly), real-time feedback opportunities, and using data to build collaborations between colleagues best suited to solving a problem and making decisions (wherever they are in the business).

That individual experience must be built on something genuine and substantive. Plenty of firms have created posts for diversity and inclusion officers, but if this isn't matched by satisfactory improvements in the steps a firm actually takes to further this agenda, stakeholders will see straight through it. As Doug McMillon, CEO of Walmart, admitted when questioned about the firm in light of the Black Lives Matter protests:

> *We have had a focus for a long time on diversity and inclusion... but we are not as diverse as we want to be and aspire to be, and that's something that we're working on.*[204]

Nike's tale of woe is instructive. The firm had become synonymous with leadership on social justice through its marketing campaigns, which famously included one featuring the American footballer Colin Kaepernick, who caused widespread controversy by 'taking the knee' to protest police brutality in the United States.

But, having been thrust into the spotlight, the firm was hit with accusations that its external brand did not reflect its internal workings. Not long after, the firm's director of diversity and inclusion stepped down, to be replaced by the new role of chief talent, diversity and culture officer. Chief Executive John Donahoe wrote to staff to say:

> *You have told me that we have not consistently supported, recognised and celebrated our own black teammates in a manner they deserve. This needs to change.*[205]

Nike clearly saw the moral imperative to act and it has, to date, been effective. The firm recently reported an increased number of people from marginalised backgrounds, which they call 'U.S. underrepresented groups', in VP-level positions. The figure is now 21%.[206]

However, morality cannot, be the sole incentive for firms looking to truly embrace inclusion and diversity. Rightly or wrongly, this becomes a much more powerful concept when it is paired with a financial incentive – just as we saw with BlackRock and sustainability. Fortunately, that financial incentive is well established. If it were not, then Goldman Sachs wouldn't have announced in 2020 that it would no longer arrange IPOs for companies with all-male, all-white boards.[207] Goldman's Chief Executive David Solomon told the World Economic Forum in Davos:

> *I look back at IPOs over the last four years and the performance of IPOs where there's been a woman on the board in the US is significantly better than the performance of IPOs where there hasn't been a woman on the board.*[208]

Boston Consulting Group's research is a case in point; it found companies with diverse management teams boasted 19% higher 'innovation revenues'.[209] Similarly, a report from McKinsey & Company suggests that corporations in the top 25% for the number of women on their executive team were '21% more likely to have above-average profitability' than those in the bottom 25%.[210] Moreover, they were '27% more likely… to have industry-leading performance on longer-term value creation'.[211] In all these examples we are looking at great gains for embracing diversity in its most basic forms. Imagine what we could achieve if we were able to attract and nurture diversity in all the forms we discussed before?

We shouldn't be sitting around waiting to find out, that's for sure. Customer expectations and both financial and regulatory pressure will drive organisations to better reflect the societies and customers they serve. On a purely practical level, the case for diversity (in all its forms) will grow stronger and stronger as 4IR demands new skillsets that simply won't be available unless firms cast the net wide. As we will see in the X-Factor chapter, there is then an even greater prize to be won when you bring these skills together to foster connected thinking and super charge innovation in your organisation. Those in learning functions have a major role to play in leveraging data and facilitating conversations that will engage leaders, inform the decision-making, and prompt action in this area.

One big caveat: beware simply falling back on the traditional route of trying to improve the skillsets of previously under-served groups. John Amaechi, a former NBA basketball player and organisational psychologist, has a powerful message for those looking to drive positive action in the area of diversity and inclusion. He believes that 'We need to stop armouring minorities with education and instead de-weaponise the cultures that we oversee'.[212]

This requires putting a greater focus on addressing the organisational cultures that are holding minority groups back. Amaechi believes firms need to put more weight on teaching values, rather than focusing simply on the technical, compliance and governance learning that might boost a single person's career:

> *We need to stop looking at this as a deficit model – black people aren't broken, women aren't broken, people with disabilities and impairments aren't broken. The environment they are in is toxic.*[213]

A crucial driver of this change will be transparency, something that firms will have forced upon them if they don't address it on their own terms. Employees, investors, suppliers, regulators and other groups are demanding more information and if it is not forthcoming through official channels, there's a good chance the data in other ways. In the words of Trevor Phillips OBE, founding chair of the UK's Equality and Human Rights Commission:

Transparency is the key to changing the culture of organisations and industries. Companies today are like glass boxes; yes they post their values, vision statements and purpose. But we can see what they are like, through social media. Whistle-blowers tell us what it is really like inside the organisation. Their annual reports and the analytics and data show the demographics in terms of diversity, inclusion and culture; who is in which roles and paid what. We can see if what they say and do are the same.

Going hand-in-hand with these greater levels of transparency comes an increasing need for colleagues at all levels to have a voice and be listened to. This comes back to Vernã Myers' point around being asked to dance, rather than just being invited to the event. Rather than stifle this voice, you should do whatever you can to encourage individuals to speak up – and then listen to them and analyse what they are saying. The notion that workers have nothing useful to contribute to management belongs to the 19th Century, not the 21st. The front line is often a hotbed of innovation and great ideas, if they can flourish.

This is an obvious area where learning professionals should be taking the lead. This is all about listening, educating, ensuring the right plans are in place, and that there is accountability and ownership, right up to C-Suite level. The case for a strategic focus on inclusion and diversity should be simple to make: it will ensure you have the right talent in place to maximise the opportunity for the organisation to reach its business goals and fulfil its purpose. It is also quite easy to measure, based on employee feedback. Diversity and inclusion is often reflected in high levels of trust and the perception of having a voice that is listened to. These are indicators of belonging, inclusion and employee engagement.

However, none of this can be achieved without clarity around organisational culture and purpose, and without putting the right learning and people strategies in place, supported by appropriate systems and processes throughout the employee lifecycle. In other words, it can't be done without you.

Your first job then is to collect as much hard evidence as you can to identify gaps and shine a light on disparities. This will help you understand people's lived experiences at all levels of the organisation. With sensitivity as your watchword, this is about encouraging people to join the conversation of change. It may also mean collecting data on characteristics that might be more difficult to quantify, including faith and sexual orientation. This is particularly true where individuals face discrimination and disadvantages. The challenges or prejudices people face can be complex. For example, Kevin has a colleague who identifies as a woman, as well as being a lesbian, and having ADHD (Attention Deficit Hyperactivity Disorder). These overlapping identities are often called intersectionality.

But the more data you have, the more you will be able to have courageous conversations facilitate discussions around privilege, create awareness, make the best decisions at all levels of the business, and – crucially – measure the impact of changes. The last thing people need is unconscious bias training that is seen as a token exercise, after which people go back to their normal lives.

EXPECTATION THREE: A GLOBAL, MULTI-GENERATIONAL WORKPLACE

The business world continues to globalise. Changes in urbanisation, demographics, health and wealth mean organisations are searching ever further afield for talent to fill skill gaps, as they prepare for our technologically integrated future.

With the increased employee expectation of flexibility in where, when and how people work, opportunities for dispersed teams have increased. With so many more people working from home it has become clear to even the staunchest traditionalists that work can – and possibly should – be done from anywhere in the world that is convenient and productive. Companies now need to go further and make sure these opportunities are available all the way up and down the hierarchy, if they are to address and embrace diversity, and retain high-performing talent.

As we have already seen in 'Adaptability', people are being asked to collaborate more quickly and to solve ever more complex problems. 'Swarm', or 'surge' teams are being quickly and systematically brought together to deliver a strategic objective or solve a problem. They exist for short periods and then disband.[214] Done well, the person in the team best equipped to lead takes charge (rather than the most senior). Phenomena like swarm teams mean cross-functional working and skills will become ever more important, while structures and processes must exist to facilitate them, no matter where their members might be in the world.

The problem is many organisations still operate in the kind of departmental and geographical silos that make such organic, fluid teams impossible. Those tasked with learning and development will need to take a leading role in re-examining and breaking down rigid structures to facilitate collaboration and reap the benefits of a global workforce.

Organisations can benefit hugely from seeking global talent pools, but there is also a crucial function this strategy can facilitate on behalf of wider society. We have spoken a lot about the benefits 4IR will bring, but there is also a real risk that the economic rewards of this new era could become highly concentrated among a small group. If this happens there is the threat of political polarisation, a collapse of trust in institutions, and social fragmentation.

As such, organisations may have a practical, competitive need to source the best talent, but can also perform a higher purpose by ensuring a more even spread of skills, opportunities and rewards across the globe. In doing so, they might help avoid some of the widely touted negative consequences of 4IR.

Another double-edged sword is the benefit that 4IR brings in terms of health and lifestyle. As life expectancy increases we are going to be working longer and workplace dynamics will have to change as a result. We could soon see *five generations* working side-by-side – that's more than at any time in human history and means a lot more support will be needed to enable these generations to work together, be productive, and remain healthy.

- Traditionalists – born 1925 to 1945.
- Baby Boomers – born 1946 to 1964.
- Generation X – born 1965 to 1980.
- Millennials – born 1981 to 1996.
- Generation Z – born 1997 to 2012.

Each generation brings different challenges and opportunities, but it falls on the organisation to understand, as best it can, the needs and values of a growing number of groups in the workplace and, hence, make the most of their skills and talents.

This cultural phenomenon could present difficulties for those who have spent many years working within more traditional hierarchical structures. These structures have long been a school of thought that equates 'time spent' with 'value'. This conclusion might well have been accurate pre-4IR – or, more likely before the Third Industrial Revolution – when change was more incremental and younger employees were often in situ to learn the skills and gain the experience of those who came before them.

The rapid change in technology and society in the last few years has destroyed that natural – and perhaps comfortable – hierarchy, particularly in more innovative firms. These days, senior staff can easily find themselves well versed in strategy, tactics, and delivery methods that are becoming obsolete. They might have spent years in a certain industry but a new-joiner – souped-up on digital innovation – might offer solutions they could never conceive of. Expertise is the not preserve of older workers in the way it once was. Of course, there is no substitute for the industry experience and maturity essential for some roles – and this only comes with time – but expertise cannot and should not be measured or valued in such a simplistic way.

Right now, there are people coming into the workplace – perhaps for the first time – who are digital natives that, despite their young age, will be able to teach the CEO a thing or two about tech, as well as consumer trends, tastes and expectations. Fashion brand Gucci created a 'shadow board' for exactly this reason.[215] It is a prime example of a firm recognising and taking advantage of this non-traditional approach to 'expertise' and we will look at this case study in more detail in the X-Factor section of CAPEX.

As Gucci shows, we are not talking about subverting entire and established leadership hierarchies, we are talking about a new willingness to accept that expertise can be found throughout your organisation and that it should be leveraged to inform and enhance the value proposition of your business. If you can put the systems and processes in place to seek out and make use of that expertise, you will demonstrate clear strategic value.

It is important to note that the notion of acceptance cuts both ways. Young, digital natives are often touted as the 'future', but they don't hold all the answers, not least because there aren't enough of them. The world's population is expected to reach 8.5bn by 2030, up from 7.3bn in 2015.[216] Of course, given the natural ageing process, it is clear that the Millennial and Gen Z generations will increasingly dominate the workforce. Even so, the fastest growing demographic *overall* will be the very elderly population who they are replacing.[217]

The population of people over 65-years-old is estimated to reach one billion by 2030.[218] Workforce demographics will have to change, with those over 65 working longer and gaining new skills as they do.[219] If organisations don't adapt then elder generations will put an enormous financial burden on the younger ones, who would otherwise need to support a growing number of retirees – and there is no logical reason why this should happen.[220]

Celebrating a 100th birthday used to be rare. Not so now. One clear demonstration of this is how countries recognise their centenarians. In Japan, reaching a 100th birthday once meant the gift of a solid silver cup from the Prime Minister.[221] In the UK, the same event elicited a message of congratulation from the monarch.[222] Today, living for 100 years is so common in Japan that the cup is now only silver plated, as it became too expensive to stick with the solid silver version.[223] In the UK, the number of people employed to send the monarch's cards has risen from one to seven.[224]

As of 2000, half or more of the children born in many wealthy countries were predicted to live for 100 or more years should present trends continue.[225] Were they instead born in England between 1901–10, they could have expected to live to around 50 – half the figure at the turn of the millennium![226] What's more, these extra years will likely be healthy, as morbidity rates decrease in many parts of the world.

Organisations will need to think a good deal harder about how they keep these experienced and talented colleagues engaged and still learning.

In *The 100-Year Life*, psychologist Lynda Gratton and economist Andrew Scott argue that increased longevity will impact workplaces in several specific ways. They predict that people will:[227]

1. Continue working into their 70s and 80s
2. Transition between jobs many different times during their lives, meaning that they will need to undertake continuous education
3. Live a less structured life, that encompasses multiple jobs, periods in education, mid-life career breaks, and working flexibility beyond the normal retirement age

This is not something that should be seen as being 'imposed' on older workers. Work helps give us a sense of purpose and of worth. It can help keep people healthier too, a key factor when we consider the impact ageing populations will have on health systems. As such, it is hardly surprising that, in the UK, over half of those aged 65 to 69 and almost 20% of those aged 70 to 74 are expected to be working by 2067.[228]

While organisations must embrace multi-generational workforces, it is also crucial not to categorise and homogenise these different groups by ascribing certain characteristics to each. It is all too easy for those across the human resources profession, as well as industry leaders, to get distracted by the perceived needs of each individual generation. There is simply too much crossover to do this. It is much better – and easier – to focus on what they have in common when aligning organisational culture and purpose with the needs of the workforce. Doing this will also offer a clear framework for delivering their learning needs.

In their book *The Best Team Wins: The New Science of High Performance*, Adrian Gostick and Chester Elton argue the Millennial (or Generation Y), Generation X and Baby Boomer generations share three top motivators. All three generations want:[229]

- to have an impact
- to learn
- to achieve work-life balance.

These groups also agree that:[230]

- money is their least important motivator
- learning is the most important motivation.

You need to propagate a simple mantra that age diversity is key to successful teams and businesses. People of different age groups can bring different skillsets, but also share many values and motivators that can be leveraged to drive a business forward.

At the same time, organisations need to be sensitive to what different groups expect as the quality of their performance and their productivity levels might depend on it. Research shows the youngest working generation, Gen Z – those born 1997–2012[231] – have a higher tolerance for workplace pressure (no matter what you might have heard). Conversely, seven out of ten Millennials (1981–1996) complain of burnout at work, according to Gallup[232] – and employees who complain of burnout are 63% more likely to take a sick day.[233]

It has never been more important for businesses and society to think creatively about how to leverage this diversity. It is up to those responsible for learning to promote greater understanding of the individual and their strengths, and to help colleagues to see what they have in common and how their differences can be complementary.

ONE THING TO UNITE THEM ALL

There are so many different elements to consider when it comes to the changing expectations of the 4IR workplace that adapting to them might seem daunting, or even downright baffling. But there is one common ingredient that pulls all this together and will be your greatest ally on this journey. That element is trust. If we are to embrace diversity in all its facets and on a global scale; if we are to meet people's expectations of personal flexibility and empowerment in work; if we are to create values-led, purpose-driven cultures and caring work environments then high levels of trust will be essential in our organisations.

That trust will come if we create that consumer-like personalised learning experience, which is inclusive, equitable and makes people feel they belong regardless of their background, generation or global location. It will come if we focus on what we have just seen to be in common, that is:

- to have an impact
- to learn
- to achieve work-life balance.

If we do this we will make our employees happy. In a workplace environment it is all too easy to get used to being unhappy and believe it to be the price one has to pay for success (or even just picking up our pay). This isn't good for health and wellbeing and, ultimately as we saw in culture, it is unsustainable and bad for the business.

Mohammad 'Mo' Gawdat is the former Chief Business Officer for Google X, Google's secret innovation lab responsible for many of its biggest breakthroughs. He is also the author of *Solve for Happy*. Mo says happiness occurs when events in your life meet or exceed your expectations.[234] Unhappiness, on the other hand, is when your life and experiences fall below your expectations.[235]

In the swirling world of 4IR, where expectations are constantly changing and being challenged by the rapidly changing environment, it will become increasingly important that learning opportunities are in place to exceed your employee and customer expectations. Not delivering on this could have severe ramifications for any firm as, rather than thrive, in this new world of work, businesses will sink under the growing weight of their experiences not meeting their employees' expectations.

CAPEX – 'X' IS FOR X-FACTOR

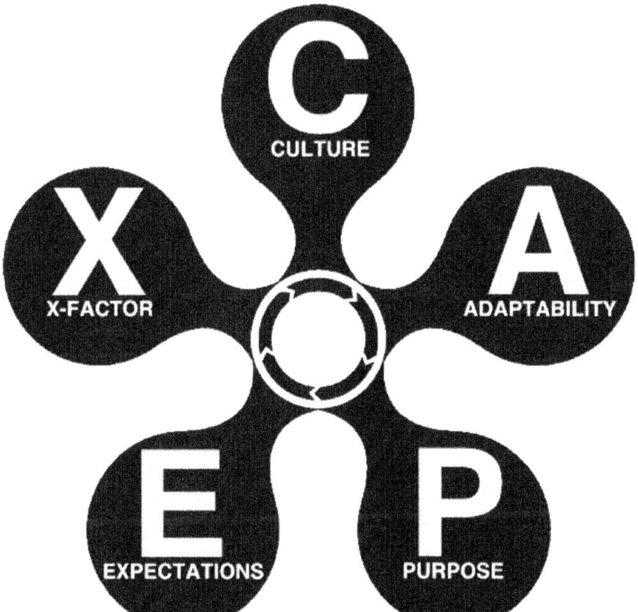

Every organisation is looking for the X-Factor: that intangible quality that drives innovation and creativity, delivering amazing products, services, customer engagement and so on. Companies like Apple, Google and Amazon are among those who seem to have captured those elusive virtues and deliver them effortlessly. It seems X-Factor is a part of their DNA. But all firms are going to have to discover this apparently magical quality if they want to fully recognise the benefits of the Fourth Industrial Revolution. 4IR is a minefield that will require firms to be ready for many possible futures, to be able to adapt and, if necessary, reset the direction of any given part of their business. Fostering the X-Factor is crucial to pulling this off.

Those looking jealously at firms like Amazon and Apple ask: where does it come from and what drives it? Is it the best talent? Is it your organisational culture? Or is it something else? Can you capture it in your organisation? If so, how? Will acting like a trendy tech firm and installing a slide, ball pit, or ping-pong table in the foyer help? Or is it a random and indiscriminate gift that somehow emerges by luck or through the nature of the work you do? And, if that is so, do I have to accept it is just something a firm is somehow born with? Happily, the answer as to whether you can find and cultivate your own X-Factor is a resounding 'Yes'!

At the core of the X-Factor lies creativity and innovation. These might sound like chaotic concepts born of flashes of genius, but they are nothing of the sort. They can be created, harnessed, and nurtured. The key is to know what elements you need to put in place for them to flourish and the right learning techniques to apply. After all, 'necessity is the mother of invention'.[236] When the need for something becomes essential, you are forced to find ways of attaining or achieving it. The rapid changes we have seen over the last few years has thrown much of the research and thinking on creativity and innovation up in the air.

The research in question focuses on the need for time and effort for creative thought, design and turning ideas into innovation. However, the pandemic proved we can innovate faster than we thought when circumstances dictate.

While causing terrible damage to economies and populations, COVID-19 did, ironically, accelerate our application of innovation and our journey into 4IR. Take the imposition of social distancing and the solutions companies have found to facilitate that in their operations, many of which have the stamp of 4IR all over them. In the countries as diverse as US[237] and Columbia,[238] companies have rolled out food delivery robots, while Singapore used a robot dog called 'Spot' to patrol parks, reminding visitors to maintain social distancing.[239] Pan-European supermarket chain Lidl has offered customers a WhatsApp chatbot that uses 'real time *[sic]* data and customer transaction numbers' to reveal the quietest – and safest – visiting times.[240] Elsewhere, fashion brand Diesel launched a 360-degree 'selling platform' and virtual showroom – the kind of solution bricks and mortar stores have been wrestling unsuccessfully with for years as they fight to combat a drop in footfall.[241]

But solutions don't necessarily require advanced tech. Connected thinking can allow you to pivot quickly, as evidenced by Selecta, a provider of vending machines. During the pandemic, it repurposed – and, importantly, rebranded – its vending machines as 'Safety Stations' that provided masks, sanitiser, and other essentials for travellers at railway stations and airport.[242] Others looked back in time for inspiration. Drive-in cinemas and concerts – reminiscent of 1950s America – sprung up around the world, where audience members simply turn up to the gig in their cars and park in rows. The soundtrack is broadcast through via their FM radios.[243]

The lesson is that when the chips are down, leaders and organisations are perfectly able to quickly assess new circumstances, recognise patterns and opportunities, quickly change directions, restructure and refocus – when necessity requires it. In other words, they discovered their X-Factor. We need to make the case to our organisations that this will become the new normal as 4IR progresses and we should be looking to (re)focus our learning programmes to encourage and facilitate it. That focus can be targeted in three areas, in a similar manner to how we approached both Purpose and Expectations. Those areas are the promotion of organisational, team, and personal X-Factor.

ORGANISATIONAL X-FACTOR

CREATING AN X-FACTOR CULTURE

Tim Brown, CEO of design and consulting firm IDEO believes that innovation – whether it is used for improving a process or for solving a big problem like making your organisation carbon neutral – can be achieved if people have the freedom to explore, experiment, and take risks. If your colleagues are afforded this flexibility they can (and will) design effective solutions for nearly any problem. In Brown's words:

> *The faster we make our ideas tangible, the sooner we will be able to evaluate them, refine them, and zero in on the best solution.*[244]

All this starts with enabling leaders to practice creative leadership. Creative leadership isn't about having all the ideas, it is about creating a culture where ideas are valued and everyone is willing and able to share. It is about deliberately creating opportunities and time for people to innovate; it is about making people feel they are free to speak their minds openly in a safe environment. It is about encouraging employees to speak out about issues beyond their own roles as part of a culture of improvement and opportunity.

If you foster a culture where people have the structures, opportunities and time to learn and think creatively, innovative ideas will flow. You need to develop leadership so it becomes a conduit for social interaction and allowing people to experiment. Organisations that persist with a more command and control version of leadership are encouraging a culture that says, 'Follow me and do what I tell you'. Often the X-Factor wilts and dies in such an environment.

But creating such a learning climate – and thus developing the leadership capability that facilitates and drives innovation – is only the first step. All creativity is moot if decisions cannot be made on how to leverage the ideas it generates. Ideas are great, but turning them into tangible innovation is the decisive test. The buck still needs to stop somewhere.

These times of unprecedented change are ripe for creating innovative environments, but they also offer leaders the toughest test of their decision-making expertise ever. Many leaders are not – or at least do not feel – equipped to make such decisions. You can change that if you foster an organisation that has a clear focus on performance improvement and the problem at hand, but also allows leaders to fail fast and to adapt as they learn from their experiences. You need to make sure success is well-publicised and human stories are built around these victories that create an emotional connection to people. If you do this you will start to create a movement that will gain momentum and build a culture of creativity among colleagues at all levels of the organisation. We will go more deeply into creating movements shortly.

TEAM X: THE POWER OF COLLABORATION

No matter what you hear, creativity is a team sport. Innovative technological and scientific breakthroughs throughout history are often perceived as being achieved by isolated individuals, often caricatured as mad scientists or brainy computer geeks. This is a myth. Take these rather impressive historical figures who weren't the lone geniuses they are often touted to be.

Albert Einstein published his general theory of relativity in November 1915. This landmark discovery is often described as Einstein's brainchild and his alone. The reality is he received a massive amount of help, input and insights from colleagues and friends, most of whom never rose to prominence, and were forgotten over time.[245]

Let us stay with science for a moment because it offers us a great template for effective collaboration and innovation. Science is all about pushing boundaries and making discoveries. As such, the mental drivers required to dream big and bring about change are just the beginning of the process. The whole philosophy of scientific investigation then requires every idea to go through collaboration, scrutiny and validation to create a better product or solution. It can't be done alone and it can't be done without the wisdom of crowds (as small as they might be) if any form of innovation is to prove sustainable. This is the kind of creative rigour you need to instil if you are not just to breed the X-Factor, but to harness its power effectively.

At the other end of the technological scale, Steven Johnson notes that when humans first began to organise themselves into settlements, towns and cities, they became members of networks, which exposed them to new ideas and allowed them to spread their own discoveries.[246] Before this happened, a novel idea by one person could well die with him or her, since she had no network within which to spread it.[247] Great ideas always have been – and always will be – born and raised in crowds. We need to encourage and facilitate collaboration if we want to develop creativity and innovation.

David Allen put it nicely when he said, 'Your mind is for having ideas, not for holding them'.[248] Once you have an idea, share it – and encourage others to share theirs – otherwise it will do nothing but drain energy and take away focus.

There are no boundaries to how far you can go to harness the team dynamic to promote innovation. Bringing together diverse teams to solve strategic problems is a massive opportunity to accelerate innovation and performance. Success might come from a regional office, an inter-departmental team, or from whole industries coming together to get creative.

The latter was ably demonstrated during 2020 when the economic impact of the pandemic led to airlines, hotels and retailers making thousands of people redundant. In China, a collaboration of more than 40 companies created an exchange to combat this trend.[249] On one side of the exchange were companies like cinemas, hotels, and restaurants, which had all taken a significant economic hit. On the other side were booming retailers. Innovative, flexible strategies like this – borne of both necessity and creativity – are likely to increasingly become the norm as 4IR progresses.

PERSONAL X-FACTOR

FINDING THE PATTERNS

We've taken a top down approach to the X-Factor so far in this chapter, as starting with the organisation as an entity and working downwards is important in ensuring both teams and individuals are working within an organisational structure that not only promotes creativity and innovation, but also shapes it in a coherent way. But we must be wary that infrastructure does not become more than a guiding star and turns into something altogether more restrictive. The culture we foster, and the processes and structures we put in place, should serve one purpose: to bring the X-Factor out in each individual person.

But just what is personal 'X-Factor' and does everyone have it? Futurists are a good place to start when examining something as intangible sounding as this. We're not talking about crystal ball gazing here. We're talking about people being able to research and recognise trends and then use those trends to paint a picture of the future. This approach is a key part of the X-Factor puzzle because basing your understanding of the future on as many data points as possible is what lets businesses bring the future to life now. Or, more accurately, it gives *people* the ability to see more clearly; to be more creative and innovative; to leverage their own X-Factor. As futurist Thomas Frey says:

> *People's vision of the future, and what the future holds, is what drives their decisions today. Their images of the future change the decisions of today.*

If you give people access to data and trends – or teach them how to go looking and what to look for – they will be able to see more clearly into the future. In doing so, you allow the future to drive our decisions today, rather than the other way around.

The key to doing this as accurately and effectively as possible is to promote the application of an open mind. In *Superforecasting: The Art and Science of Prediction*, authors Philip Tetlock and Dan Gardner say that the best performing 'superforecasters' are those that explore insights from multiple sources and from different viewpoints.[250] It is also important to keep re-examining these insights and adjust predictions incrementally as new data or circumstances emerge to do this you require connected thinking.

These data points can come from almost anywhere. They will come from individual research and they will come from collaboration. Innovators learn from a diverse range of people and organisations with in-depth knowledge of the trends, issues, problems and opportunities. They also need access to a diverse range of people who can offer more than technical knowledge, including insights into behaviour, culture and many other things.

These voices will offer challenges and affirmation from different viewpoints and could come from anywhere in the organisation – from the shop floor to the boardroom. It is up to you to foster a culture that encourages this desire for knowledge and offers the opportunity to speak up, to challenge and to be heard.

You must also embrace the data yourself to make sure you have – and will have – the people and the skills that will serve your organisation going forward. There is no shortage of big data, trends and collective intelligence out there to help us formulate that vision. You can look at elements that are specific to your industry and you can look at macro trends that will impact us all.

Let us remind ourselves of the research we referenced previously from McKinsey, the Harvard Business Review, Deloitte, and the World Economic Forum (amongst others), which suggests that, in general, the top five skills that will be required among employees to make an organisation thrive as 4IR progresses are:

- creativity and critical/connected thinking

- resilience and navigating through uncertainty
- collaboration and trust
- complex problem solving and decision-making
- influence and persuasion.

These skills could be called the innovators skill-set and will sit at the heart of driving creativity and innovation in the 4IR. But to foster these skills, we first need the right mindset.

THE INNOVATOR'S MINDSET

An innovator is someone who starts as a pioneer – in that they see potential where others do not – and who is then willing to go ahead and try new things. They push boundaries to advance a cause or an idea. To be like this requires a particular mindset, which starts with critical thinking. By that we mean the objective analysis and evaluation of an issue to make an informed judgement. Be careful, though, that 'critical' is not misinterpreted as a reason to tell people everything is wrong and we are all doomed!

But there's another level of thinking that lies at the heart of critical thinking and differentiates true innovators from the wannabes. This is the skill we need to develop in our organisations, in our colleagues and leaders at all levels if we are to innovate and be ready for the future.

This higher level is called connected thinking. When innovators talk about connected thinking they regularly explain it in terms of joining up or connecting the dots. They seem to have this incredible ability to find hidden patterns and make connections that other people do not see, often in seemingly unrelated things.

This trait is not new. Creativity expert Michael Michalko sets out just how far Leonardo da Vinci would go to connect the unconnected. He suggested that you will find inspiration for marvellous ideas if you look into the stains on walls, or ashes of a fire, or the shape of clouds or patterns in mud or in similar places. He would imagine seeing trees, battles, landscapes, figures with lively movements, etc... and then excite his mind by forcing connections between the subjects and events he imagined and his subject.[251]

More recently, Sir Richard Branson famously said his mantra for success in his Virgin companies was: A+B+C+D (Always Be Connecting the Dots).[252] This involves reshaping dispersed and discontinuous information for innovative purposes.[253]

Clayton Christensen is a Harvard Business School professor best known for his book, *The Innovator's Dilemma* and himself a case study for connected thinking. He created and pioneered the concept of disruptive innovation.[254] This is 'a process whereby a smaller company... is able to successfully challenge established incumbent businesses'.[255] Karen Dillon, former editor of the *Harvard Business Review* marvelled at how he would connect dots that others couldn't even see. She put it down to one key element:

> *For Clay, it was all about asking the right questions. To Clay, a great question was worth more than a great answer. Because without the great question, we would never get to the right answer.*[256]

This book is the result of connected thinking. It is the result of looking at many, seemingly disconnected behaviours, trends, and schools of thought, and then finding patterns and interconnectivities between them. Those patterns produced the CAPEX formula and now it is your turn to take this formula and promote connected thinking in your own organisation. And it is worth starting with the fact that the way we are often asked to learn is not conducive to this crucial skill.

Marketing guru Seth Godin has complained that schools students learn all about 'collecting dots', but aren't taught much about 'connecting' them.[257] When it does happen, Godin says it is like magic:

> *Once you learn the techniques, the dots can change but you'll still be good at connecting them.*[258]

This assertion is borne out by Peter Fisk in his book, *Gamechangers.*[259] He asked 1,000 CEOs whom they thought were the most innovative companies. He then looked in-depth at the top 100, which spread across ten sectors. The primary insight he got from this was all these firms shaped the market to their advantage. They didn't see innovation as designing a new product or services, they were asking themselves how they innovate the market space and mould it. They reframed the space they were in to find new competitors or change the perceived value of what they offer. Others were then finding they were forced to innovate in their business as a response to the innovation of the market.

Mr Fisk says the market is changing so fast that you can shape it to your advantage.[260] He says the most innovative companies see the malleability of markets and design a future they can be successful in. But to do this the crucial thing is to 'see the dots others don't see'.[261]

If you can take these dots and connect them – or, in the case of learning, encourage and facilitate others to do so – you can achieve amazing things. Tarana Burke's creation of #MeToo, the movement against sexual harassment, assault and misconduct is one example. In her words:

> *If we don't talk about eliminating sexual harassment in the workplace, then it hinders the conversation around ending sexual harassment in the street or in schools... People don't understand that allowing sexual harassment to thrive creates a culture and opens up space for sexual violence to happen. That has been my goal in this moment – to give some context to it and allow people to connect the dots. It's all related.*[262]

If we can help people in our organisations to develop their connected thinking then we can help them set their thinking free from the constraints of traditional, structured thinking that is fraught with limitations we are not even aware of. In the words of connected thinking expert Faisal Hoque, this means 'connecting the dots between our emotional selves and systematic thinking'.[263] Do this and you will see an explosion of creativity and innovation in your organisation. You will unleash the X-Factor.

LEARNING TO JOIN THE DOTS

Pattern recognition and connected thinking is a skill we all have. If we want to develop it, we need focus, practice, and have the capacity to take a step back. Firstly, it is important to realise your brain is on your side here. Your brain is wired to recognise patterns and to connect dots. In its most basic (but arguably most important) form, pattern recognition enabled our ancestors to survive, allowing them to distinguish predator from prey and identify poisonous from sustaining plants. It is pattern recognition that allowed our ancestors to learn about the environment they were living in, and to make predictions and take decisions that helped them survive and thrive. Today, pattern recognition is just as important in a multitude of areas: from diagnosing diseases, to inspiring new ways to safeguard data from cyber-attack, and starting new social movements.[264]

It is grasping patterns that gives us a sense of order in what might otherwise appear a complex and chaotic landscape. Understanding and being able to identify recurring patterns makes learning easier, allowing us to be more strategic and make decisions that are quicker and better informed.

The brain rewards those practising pattern learning. Ian Krajbich, assistant professor of psychology and economics at Ohio State University, has done extensive research on how the brain connects patterns. He and a colleague at the University of Zurich discovered that when participants found connections in the tests he ran, a separate part of the brain was activated, alongside that which made the connections. This was the ventromedial prefrontal cortex – a part of the brain that is linked to reward.[265] This suggests our brain actively encourages us to notice patterns by giving us a sense of achievement when we do.[266] There are important ramifications from this discovery, in terms of learning: not only does promoting this pattern recognition – or connecting the dots – align strongly with the skills we need in 4IR, it naturally fuels our desire to learn the skills we need.

The imperative to promote connected thinking is made all the stronger when we consider how heavily *not* doing it will weigh on people and organisations in the context of 4IR. If, during your job, you are expected to be increasingly creative and innovative to thrive in the new world, an inability to effectively process ever more complex forms of data will limit your potential and productivity, and lead to several unpleasant side effects.

Human beings naturally seek to understand, predict and control – it helps us learn and it keeps us safe. Uncertainty can feel dangerous because we cannot confidently predict what will happen. Such uncertainty – particularly over an extended period – seriously affects our performance, decision-making and, most importantly, our mental health. As such, embedding connected thinking in our organisations will help both people and businesses to thrive during the oncoming times of uncertainty. It will help us adapt, be resilient and have a sense of control while the winds of change whistle around us.

One caveat here is around unconscious bias, where people favour others who look like them and/or share their values because they attribute certain underlying attitudes and stereotypes to another person or group of people. This can create patterns and build associations where none belong. A key part of effective connected thinking – and thus optimising the opportunity and innovation – is the need to consciously analyse the dots we have joined and gain different perspectives from different people. Once again, we are taken back to history's great innovators – from Einstein to Newton and beyond – and reminded that great innovation almost never happens in a vacuum. Our teams and our networks will be crucial to ensuring we avoid this unconscious bias.

And so we begin to see that creativity and innovation – for all its reputation of being based in outbursts of spontaneous inspiration – is actually based on solid foundations of research and understanding of trends, markets, audiences, and other factors. Using this approach means we can start to plan for, and develop, the skills our firms will need for the future in a controlled, yet agile way.

This is one of the reasons why there has been a movement towards learning within the flow of work 2.0 – real-time learning. To develop creative skills, people need hands-on experiences that develop their wider skillset, rather than simply learning theory in a Google search, TED Talk or classroom session and hoping it is applied. That's why we're so keen on advocating this structured approach to identifying the performance improvement the business requires, the problem they want to solve, or the customer value they can add and deliberately building in the time and space for people to learn whilst in the flow of working on the strategic objective.

Step forward the learning professional… no one is better placed to see the big picture and then take the steps needed to help colleagues to solve their business challenges. These steps can help solve big ticket business challenges, as well as improve daily performance through incremental and continuous improvement. Traditional learning and development isn't enough, you have to get ahead and understand the latest technology and also allow people to solve business problems whilst learning from experience.

REAL-TIME LEARNING

At the core of developing the X-Factor in a holistic way across your organisation – that is, at organisational, team, and individual levels – lies in the six pillars of real-time learning. These are designed to help get those creative juices flowing and deliver results.

PILLAR ONE – IDENTIFYING AND ADDRESSING A COMPLEX PROBLEM

Firstly, you need to be clear on the problem you want to solve or the performance you want to improve and why. With rampant change and technological developments all around us, there is more opportunity than ever to find yourself in possession of a solution that needs a problem. You need to make sure you know what your goals are and can clearly articulate what success looks like.

This process starts with learning professionals looking to facilitate conversations that create opportunities for innovation, based on a problem or issue that the organisation is looking to solve. This might seem simple or obvious, but how often are proactive steps taken in your organisation to help colleagues be innovative and creative in their problem-solving? In *Relentless Innovation*, author Jeffrey Phillips argues that

> *We are habitually busy, and so we focus on the next activity, next day, the next fire, rather than being able to give time to issues that require deep concentration. Being mired in tasks becomes the normal thing to do. We just need some deep focus.*[267]

He also states that this lack of opportunity to be creative and innovative is exacerbated by:

- inflexible processes that allow individuals or collectives to procrastinate
- silo working that actively promotes *un*connected thinking
- different agendas or organisational politics that block or delay progress.

You need to look for these danger signs and work to break down barriers, streamline engagement processes, and unblock obstructions. At the same time, you need to remain focused on the job in hand. Real-time learning is not much use if 'creativity and innovation' and 'wacky and off-beat' become interchangeable concepts. People still need to be solving the *right* problems – by which we mean those that have meaning to the individual or organisation they aim to help and which offer you business benefit and ROI.

Let us look at one area – shadow boards – where companies have identified complex or deep-rooted problems and used creativity and collaboration to break down some of the barriers that were standing in their way.

GUCCI – WHAT THE COMPANY DID

Gucci is a byword for the latest trends and tastes in the world of fashion, but without a comprehensive transformation programme driven by CEO Mario Bizzarri, the company might have been left behind (as some rivals were) with the world rapidly embracing a digital revolution.

Gucci created a shadow board composed of colleagues working in a wide variety of roles.[268] Bizzarri called them 'the most talented people in the organisation – [and] many of them [are] very young.'[269] The board had twin goals: to develop the firm's leadership capability and to solve current and emerging business challenges.[270] Either Bizzarri, or one of his senior executives, attended each meeting, which covered the same topics as Gucci's execs were concerned with. The result was that younger participants collaborated and, it is fair to assume, learnt in a way they never would have before from their more senior mentors. But the opposite was also true: their insights also 'served as a wakeup call for the executives,' according to Bizzarri.[271]

'Gucci's sales have since grown 136%' – from €3.5bn in the 2014 financial year to €8.3bn in 2018 – 'a growth driven largely by the success of both its Internet and digital strategies.'[272] In its review of the project, Harvard Business Review contrasted the fortunes of Gucci with rival fashion house, Prada. Meanwhile, Prada's sales have dipped by 11.5%: from €3.6bn in 2014 to €3.1bn in 2018.[273] In 2017, the company admitted that it had made a mistake by being 'slow in realising the importance of digital channels and the blogging online 'influencers', which are disrupting the industry.'[274] A shadow board of digital natives would have identified these trends much sooner.

ACCOR HOTELS – WHAT THE COMPANY DID

Given the difficulty of competing against the titan that is Airbnb, Accor Hotels found themselves needing to make changes – and fast.[275] As such, senior managers requested the company's marketing department build a brand capable of catering to millennials' needs and desires.[276]

To start with, little happened. After two years, the marketing function found themselves empty-handed. Arantxa Balson, Chief Talent and Culture Officer, took on the challenge. She decided to harness the collective intelligence of the hotel group by gathering a diverse range of individuals from across the business into a shadow board.[277] The 12-person group she built was drawn from all over the world. The participants brought with them new insights and perspectives – in specific, their understanding of what it was about Airbnb that allowed the company to seize the imagination of millennials and change the hospitality market.[278]

Chief executive Sébastien Bazin says the idea came from 'observations that the majority of recent successful companies... have been created by under-35s'.[279] As such, it made sense to incorporate the source of these great ideas into the teams determining the business' direction.[280]

In 2018,[281] the group's efforts led to the birth of Jo&Joe, a 'millennial-focused hostels brand'.[282] The group subsequently invented the Accor Pass, a subscription-based service providing young people hotel rooms while they looked for long-term accommodation.[283] Both these creations have been game changers for the hotel group.

A major reason the group succeeded was that they challenged the business direction and plans, and despite the financial constraints.[284] They were encouraged to question and challenge current brand strategy, focusing on customer experience from a younger point of view.

The shadow board approach has worked for numerous other firms and can be applied in different ways to bring fresh ideas, improve diversity, improve retention among high performers, and boost transparency. At one end of the scale, the shadow board might exist to tackle a particular corporate challenge (for example, driving demand amongst a particular demographic) or, at the other, mirroring the activities of the main board, going through the same papers and agenda, then reporting back.

CASE STUDY: SANTANDER BANK AND REAL-TIME LEARNING

On our journey into the brave new world of L&D we've already encountered Robert Ashcroft, Head of Capability at Santander bank, a couple of times. We learnt how he restructured his department and created products that would meet the expectations of a modern workforce.

The driver for this was Robert's desire to provide learning experiences that fostered self-sufficiency and were integrated into colleagues' daily work. He wanted real time learning and, not only that, he wanted experiences that could go toe-to-toe with the experiences his customers had as 21st Century consumers.

To embed this new approach, Robert and his team had to help their 'customers' in the bank realise that they didn't necessarily need to go on training courses to learn.

> *We needed to move away from this chalk and talk, classroom, mindset,' says Robert. 'We needed to take people out of a sterile learning environment where we'd been trying to replicate reality with training, role plays and case studies.*

Instead the team focuses on empowering the workforce to learn each day as part of a learning experience integrated into colleagues' daily work. Bringing the learning closer to the point of performance, productivity or the innovation. Not to see learning as a separate activity from work but to solve the customer or organisational problem whilst learning.

As such, the Capability team's chief focus is to keep those using their learning products in their actual working environment, building and forging relationships with the team(s) that they work with.

The Capability team put a learning strategy in place that was made up of three stages: experience, reflection, and action.

> *We said: let's help people have an experience or learn from someone else's experience,' says Robert. 'Then let's help them with their reflection on that and what they're taking away from it and, finally, let's encourage them to take a course of action.*

These experience–reflect–action activities are defined as 'learning sprints' by the team and designed to meet user need and foster self-sufficiency, whether that takes minutes or days of support. In this way, Robert's team can help them frame and nurture that experience, rather than imprint a text book experience.

One example of this is training for those joining the bank as mortgage advisors. Previously, new joiners would spend several weeks on a residential course before doing the job.

'Now you can join the training on any working pattern anywhere in the UK and you'll connect with my virtual coaching team and they will support you on your journey,' says Robert. 'It's very individualised, very personalised. We are no longer in this scenario where internal customers were saying, "You're giving me people after six weeks of a training who are technically compliant, but can they actually do the job?" Instead, within days, we enable learners to interact with the products and services that they're delivering to the bank's customers, in a constructive, nurturing way.'

Robert's product owners work to actively encourage people to engage in dialogue and share knowledge:

> *Our 'experience, reflection, action' process means we are expecting people to think about what they've just done or witnessed in others, have a go in testing whether that's right for them, reflect on that, then take a more formal course of action.*

> *You can read regulations, policy and procedure in a manual, but everywhere else we can we're saying, 'let's have a conversation and through that conversation share your experiences of how you and others have gone about doing something; to see what resonates with you, and whether you want to give it a go'.*

Giving feedback on performance, behaviours and skill in the moment means building individual and organisational capability and competence quicker, whilst doing something the individual cares about: their work, with the bonus of an improved employee experience too.

Real-time learning sits at the core of Robert's department's activities and delivers on their claim to have evolved from L&D to 'Capability'.

> *Learning is too synonymous with school; capability is about making people think about how they build, borrow or buy capability. I want to help colleagues answer the question 'How am I going to build capability in my team? Do I want to buy that in from the market – in terms of new hires – instead of building it? Or do I need something temporary? If I'm going to build capability, how do I do it in an accelerated fashion and ultimately get to a point where I'm retaining the capability in the organisation that we need?' If we, as a team, can do that then we're going to improve productivity, help solve complex problems, and drive a better customer experience.*

PILLAR TWO: INVOLVE THE RIGHT PEOPLE

The case studies above not only showed the value of identifying a complex issue that needs to be solved, they also clearly demonstrate that bringing the right people together stimulates and drives creativity and innovation. In 4IR, you must work to break down silos and bring people together to learn from each other, like never before. As we shall see, this means engaging with *types* of people who you might have actively avoided in the past…

The reasons the most challenging work today is undertaken in groups is simple. Firstly, these problems are too complex for any one person to tackle alone. Secondly, our brains do not operate in the same way as each other and, as such, many minds make light work. Thirdly, there are widespread knock-on benefits from bringing people together and entrusting them with solving weighty problems. It helps all those involved advance their own capabilities in connected thinking (and, ultimately, develop themselves and their careers) by offering them fresh data, perspectives and thought processes. This supports the kind of deep learning that will develop leadership capacity at all levels of an organisation and behavioural changes that will stick.

We've already looked at the importance of considering diversity in its widest form, if you want to enable collaboration in its truest sense. If you bring people together to collaborate on a problem who come from the same team and share the same knowledge and motivation, that is not effective collaboration. That is just teamwork. Collaboration is bringing different ways of thinking and different sets of knowledge and then using teamwork to get results. Real collaboration means combining different minds with different perspectives and skillsets, focusing the collective value of those involved on unusual or difficult challenges. This is where you ignite innovation.

The science of neurodiversity shows us that there are different ways the brain can work and interpret information.[285] To put it another way, people naturally think about things differently. Therefore, when we are creating a team to solve a complex problem we need to expand our definition of diversity in the widest sense. To get all the different perspectives that we need, we must also consider neurodiversity.

The benefits of considering neurodiversity are like our more standard categories because naturally diverse people are wired differently and, as such, may bring new perspectives to a company's efforts to create or recognise value. This means people who recognise themselves as having different thinking styles – such as people with autism, dyslexia, ADHD, and dyspraxia can be hugely helpful in solving problems and driving innovation. They can also bring us full circle on our earlier point about not discounting disabilities when there is a good chance that 'differently abled' is not only kinder terminology, but also more reflective of the real benefits those differences bring.

In this inclusive environment there is a particularly valuable group that you need to encourage and take care of: the rebels. Not so long ago, these people were often seen as troublemakers. This is hardly surprising when you consider they tend to be individuals who resist authority, control, and traditions – the very foundation of most businesses. As such, they stood for dissent and disorder and were generally considered a negative influence that was to be roundly discouraged.

Nowadays, these same people are often the key to unlocking creativity and driving innovation. This is because they give different perspectives, ensure we are not all thinking the same thing or in the same way, and offer a challenge to the wider status quo. In our increasingly democratised workplaces, the challenges they offer will become more apparent. These challenges can be channelled positively, or they can become destructive.

All this means rebels need to be identified and nurtured. They are a diverse group, here's a checklist of 'rebel' characteristics to help you pick them out. Rebels tend to:

- look at things differently
- prioritise what's best for people (over profit alone)
- feel suffocated by process and demand greater freedom and autonomy than their colleagues
- care more about work than your average employee
- tell the truth, even when it is unpopular
- love continuous improvements
- demand greater variety across their workplace experience

- be curious and spark off great ideas
- be future-orientated
- stand up for things they believe in
- be adaptable, flexible, and comfortable with instability
- be less afraid of risk.

The key for learning professionals is to marshal these drivers of creativity and productivity effectively. Without careful consideration, the challenge rebels offer to the status quo can become a source of resentment and adversarial behaviour.

You need to provide the opportunities for rebels to 'break' rules in ways that are positive and productive, in turn delivering new ways to optimise productivity and increase ROI.

With careful leadership and facilitation, one of the key benefits rebels offer is overcoming biases and over-compliance in teams, as they are usually the first to speak out against groupthink.

As Charlan Nemeth explains in her book, *In Defense of Troublemakers,* 'most people are afraid and they don't speak up.'[286] This is a shame, she says, as speaking up is 'a benefit regardless of whether or not dissenters hold the truth.'[287] In fact, research shows that whether a dissenter is right or wrong, they boost creativity and encourage teams to think differently.[288] The message is clear: inspire, reassure, and incite people to embrace their inner rebel and to speak up.

This brings us onto an important point about rebels: you don't have to be born a rebel, you can become one. Here are ten things learning professionals can do to encourage the mavericks and rebel talent according to Jamie Tott of Nobel Rebels:

- Value context over content and design for self-directed learning.
- Nurture individual strengths and purpose, while encouraging authenticity.
- Make it safe to challenge the status quo.
- Set challenges that stimulate constructive disobedience.

- Provoke useful collaborative action.
- Play host to initiative and conflict.
- Extend greater autonomy and trust.
- Encourage experimentation and learning from failure.
- Replace hierarchies with open networks.
- Kill rules and controls, instead favouring freedom within constraints.

You can start by applying these rules to yourself and your team. Let us not forget, this whole book is about asking you to rebel against the status quo and join the movement towards meaningful learning and work.

A final point to close this section on bringing the right people together: as these melting pots of creativity and innovation spring up, grow, and disband (as required), you will need to pay close attention to the levels of motivation that people bring to the problem or solution. The depth of emotional connection can make or break a collaboration. Bringing such diverse groups of people together can be challenging as comfort zones will be breached repeatedly. This needs to be carefully addressed as underlying all the diverse talents, experience and knowledge you are gathering must be the motivation to solve the problem at hand – or at least see the benefit in taking part in the activity.

If you find individuals who aren't motivated or just seem disinterested in the collaboration, learning professionals are in an ideal position to remedy this. Low levels of motivation tend to stem from a lack of knowledge, purpose or belief.

The solution to demotivated team members usually involves bringing the individual deeper into the conversation and offering them the opportunity to be part of something, based on a proper understanding of the business context and benefits they will gain (in terms of developing the skills and experiences that will benefit their career now, and in the future).

If you find you can't achieve these things, then you've got to ask if that person – or perhaps that project – should be there at all.

As we've already discussed, the skills required for 4IR will naturally be built through experimentation, experience, and collaborative problem solving, simply because this is an agile way to develop skills in an era that will require speed and flexibility. You don't want to find yourself surrounded by those who can't or won't engage in this agenda.

PILLAR THREE: CREATING THE DESIRED CULTURE

As a learning specialist you can make sure this holistic notion of collaboration is not only recognised, but also nurtured through the creation of just the kind of culture we've been talking about since the start: an inclusive environment that is psychologically safe; a climate in which speaking up is encouraged, enabled, and expected, where team members believe they won't be punished if you make a mistake; where you can take risks (that are proportionate to the activity) and where your opinion is valued. They will need to come together in an environment that enables and encourages creativity, openness and multiple perspectives. This will allow a free and non-judgemental flow of new ideas.

Psychological safety is crucial to this – and don't take our word for it. When the People Analytics team at Google undertook so-called Project Aristotle to discover the secrets of effective teams at the company, it found psychological safety was not just important; it was, by a clear margin, the *most* important factor in creating effective and high-performing teams.[289] On a wider front, it also helps develop the high-trust, positive, happy work culture that we've so often said will be crucial to success in 4IR.

PILLAR FOUR: CONNECTED THINKING AND DECISION-MAKING

The next – and crucial differentiator in making real-time learning a success – is for participants to be able to find patterns and notice trends in all that information and those ideas. This will help you find the big picture – a map of the salient trends in a mass of data and ideas. These ideas and trends then need to be evaluated against a set of wider parameters or goals that focuses on filtering available information, putting it in context. Next you have to make some decisions – your focus on creating a culture and environment that encourages collaboration, trust and a feeling of purpose will pay dividends here. It will allow leaders to make informed decisions and make better decisions (as well as make changes as more data and feedback becomes available). But in the fast-moving world of 4IR, they will also know that they can fail fast and adapt, promoting a culture of continuous improvement.

PILLAR FIVE: INFLUENCE AND PERSUASION

Ideas and decisions need to be justified. You will need to explain what you've done and why to stakeholders by telling your story, built on the data, processes and people that have been involved throughout the process. Storytelling skills be crucial to this and we will look at what constitutes a great story in the next chapter.

Your job is to support individuals so that they understand the big picture, have access to all the relevant data and know how to interpret it and, finally, trust their intuition (which will ultimately be shaped by the two preceding pillars). You can then work on helping colleagues to understand how to adapt the story for the different stakeholders. Reflecting on how and when to influence, persuade and take the right decisions – even in the most uncertain of times – and adapt their behaviour as required.

How you do this will be dictated by what is most appropriate in your circumstances. However, the result will be the same: you will enable colleagues to better recognise patterns and to construct ideas and innovate in ways that are business-relevant and offer both emotional meaning and functionality to those they are aimed at.

PILLAR SIX: SKILLS, BEHAVIOURS AND HABITS

You will be focused on developing the distributed leadership skills, developing resilience and the ability of navigating through uncertainty. Opportunities to reflect on learning and experiences are built into the process. Supporting participants to make sense of this learning point, helping them to reflect and to analyse it. This support can come from a peer, colleague, or coach enabling them to consciously understand what they've learnt. Each person develops a plan which must then be implemented (in collaboration with the supporter above) to help the person transfer the key moment of learning into action, behavioural change, habit or skill development over a period of time, facilitated by mutual support, encouragement, positive feedback and accountability.

This approach to developing skills will help solving some of the biggest challenges faced by your organisation and have a massive positive impact on the credibility of the learning profession. In addition to developing the X-Factor in your business, it will also remove the biggest barrier to learning – time – it also enables you to offer measurable business value and ROI for the business problem you have solved, which has been the holy grail for many years. The kind of data we can easily collect in the time of 4IR is a godsend for learning specialists trying to develop their people's skills and experiences whilst delivering on business goals.

We have now examined each of the elements of the CAPEX formula and why they are important to organisations that want to thrive in the new world of work.

- In **Culture**, we looked at organisations using their learning functions to create positive, high-performance, high-trust cultures, and what the benefits of this approach are.

- In **Adaptability** we explored the ever-greater need for organisations, teams, and individuals to be flexible, agile, responsive, resilient… and to keep things simple.
- **Purpose** lies at the heart of CAPEX, and here we looked at how aligning the 4 levels of purpose helps generate engagement, focus and commitment, and drives commercial success.
- In **Expectations** we examined how expectations (and the experiences) that people have of organisations are changing, and the opportunities this gives those responsible for learning to reinvent themselves and what they deliver.
- In **X-Factor**, we explored how you can harness the creativity, collaboration and innovation that naturally arise from harnessing the elements above to help your business evolve and thrive.

CAPEX is a process, ever-evolving and interlinked. It is never finished, but must adapt dynamically to the world we live in.

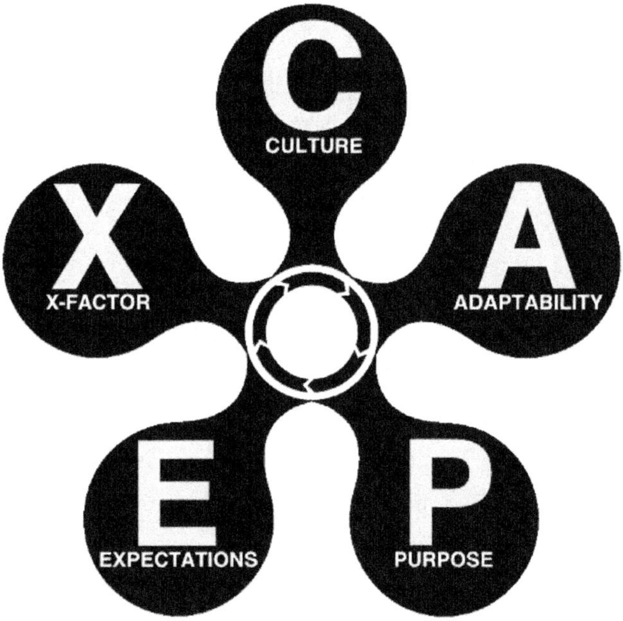

BRINGING THE CAPEX FORMULA TO LIFE IN YOUR ORGANISATION

SEIZE THE MOMENT

At this stage of the book, you may find yourself reassured that you are already on the right path and focusing on the right priorities. If, on the other hand, you haven't embarked on this journey – or if you feel you're on the wrong journey entirely – then hopefully you've seen CAPEX for what it is: a great opportunity to join a movement that is reshaping the future of work.

Hopefully both your head and your gut recognise this, based on what you've read here and on your own personal experience. If that's the case, it is time to take action and that means you've got to find the time and space to think about what happens next. Somehow you need to step away from the day job, with all its tasks, back-to-back meetings, and other complications, and identify:

- the changes you need to make
- the stakeholders you need to influence
- how you are actually going to get the ball rolling.

This might seem like a mountain to climb. It wouldn't be at all surprising if you were staring wide-eyed and asking: 'How can it be done?' The answer is to take it one step at a time.

Even if the task is mountainous, you need to think of yourself as an intrepid explorer with an exciting adventure ahead. *Really* exciting. We're looking at the biggest transformation in formal learning and development since it all started during the First Industrial Revolution back in the 18th and 19th centuries; the biggest change since mechanisation forced factory owners to give employees the knowledge and skills to work the new machinery.

The arrival of the Fourth Industrial Revolution (4IR) offers you the opportunity to become the 'cultural glue' in your organisation; to take a leading role in the evolution of your company, making it a hub of innovation and productivity where the best people want to join and stay. What an exciting time to be a learning professional!

Let us look at some of the stats so we can start our journey with a clear sense of the latent opportunity that is waiting to be tapped into:

- 42% of staff want their learning teams to create opportunities for them to learn (so there is a clear client need).[290]
- The number one reported reason for people leaving an organisation is an 'inability to learn and grow.'[291]
- Only about 20% of millennial staff 'believe they have all the skills and knowledge they'll need' for the Fourth Industrial Revolution.[292]
- 42% of millennial job applicants say an organisation's learning offering is *the* top factor when considering a new role.[293]
- As many as 48% of millennials and 36% of the general workforce would leave an employer because of poor L&D opportunities.[294]

With those happy insights putting wind in our sails, let us start the journey right now. Earlier we looked at the prevailing status quo in learning (and winced a little bit as we did so). We also looked at the business case for those willing to grasp the nettle and change the way they do business. We have looked at the CAPEX formula, which gives you a set of priorities to drive a strategic vision for the world of learning in this 4IR era. Now, we will help you either plot your course and set out on your adventure or provide focus and drive to a movement you've already started. As we do so, we will look at how you can take the CAPEX foundations and apply them to your organisation's own circumstances, get stakeholders on board with the project, and drive lasting change.

STEP ONE: RUN DIAGNOSTICS

Too often, learning professionals are so busy doing the admin and process side of the role that they do not have the time to focus on the big picture stuff: the company culture, strategic initiatives, and ways to support future plans. This needs to change. It is up to leaders like you to shake off the inhibiting legacy of learning and challenge the traditional view of the function. To create a learning environment where people to want to learn, where learning, skills and capability are being discussed at the top table. As Rob Ashcroft from Santander told us: 'Learning needs a true reinvention; a caterpillar-to-butterfly moment'. That can only happen if you step back and run a thorough diagnostic check of your function and how it operates within the context of the wider organisation.

The first thing to realise is your use of CAPEX will be unique to the business you are in. You must tailor it to the needs of your organisation. That means starting with an audit of your firm so you can work out what you should prioritise, in terms of:

- cultural development
- building adaptability
- driving purpose
- understanding peoples' expectations
- developing X-Factor.

How you do this will depend on the nature of your business, your working methods and the resources at your disposal. However, there are some key questions you can ask to frame your approach:

CULTURE

- Is your organisational culture being driven and shaped by clear organisational values?
- To what extent do you have a high-trust, positive and happy culture that ensures the wellbeing and productivity of your people? Where do you need to focus your efforts to improve this?
- Are you developing people to reflect and enhance the culture you want from the moment they join the organisation? What steps could you put in place to ensure you get the right people coming through the door, in terms of your company's marketing, job descriptions, interviews, inductions, etc?

ADAPTABILITY

- Is the range skills and talents you are prioritising and developing correct and aligned with what your company needs today and in the future?
- Do you offer clear signposting and create opportunities for colleagues to learn and develop the skills they will need for that technology-driven future?
- Are you focusing on building real-time capacity into your learning programmes to drive and enable creativity, problem solving, and innovation?
- Are you encouraging flexibility in your colleagues' outlooks, behaviours and actions, by enabling them to learn, reflect, and develop?
- Are you supporting colleagues to adapt behaviours, create habits and have an agile mind-set?
- Are the systems you are using (or building) simple and connected, so they can support a fluid and adaptive organisation?
- Is your organisational design being shaped by the skills required for the future?

PURPOSE

- Can you honestly say your organisation is purpose-driven? Does it have that aspirational reason for being, which acts as a call to action for your colleagues, partners and wider stakeholders?
- How are you supporting leaders in their role as stewards of organisational purpose and values, helping then stay true to your business's identity?
- Are you supporting colleagues to identify their own individual purpose?
- Are you promoting and integrating four levels of purpose (individual, team, organisational, and social) to drive a comprehensive approach to building a purpose-driven organisation?

EXPECTATIONS

- Do your people and culture strategies take account of, and reflect, the changing trends and expectations of consumers, employees, stakeholders and investors?
- What are you doing to develop a more human and caring workplace, where technology does not come at the expense of humanity?
- How are you harnessing diversity and inclusion in its widest sense (going beyond age, gender and race, to include cultural and social backgrounds, abilities, personalities, and even thinking styles)?
- Are you taking advantage of global talent pools?
- What mechanisms do you have in place to ensure everyone has a voice in your organisation?
- What support do you offer that enables teams to be more autonomous and/or multi-disciplinary, where needed?
- Are you engaging and facilitating a multi-generational workplace?

X-FACTOR

- How are you supporting and encouraging collaboration and innovation to solve complex problems?
- How can you simplify processes and systems to drive collaborative working?
- Are you connecting emotionally with colleagues through powerful storytelling that brings your firm's purpose, vision, mission, and values to life?
- Does your OL&D offer and support real-time learning as part of each individual's flow of work?
- Does OL&D encourage an innovative mindset by promoting connected thinking?
- Are you prioritising the skills and capabilities needed in the 4IR?
- Does your function as a whole operate on a model of data-driven decision-making and return on investment (ROI), allowing you to demonstrate the business value of your activities?
- ...If not, how can you get the support needed to turn OL&D into a function that does do that? What do you need in terms of management support, technological investment and/or financial backing?

These questions require you to look at the wider organisation and at the OL&D function itself. It is always easy to pass the blame onto the corporate structures and processes within which you operate, but change must start with you. Or to put it another way: you need to be the change that you want to see. To deliver on the promise and opportunity offered by CAPEX your own team members are going to have to upskill and reskill, and focus ruthlessly on the processes and platforms that will help you to perform. You will need to demonstrate that performance in the language of finance, economics and data analytics. To paraphrase what Herbert Gerjuoy said around 50 years ago: today and tomorrow's illiterate will not only be the ones who can't read; they will be the ones who have not learnt how to learn.

This applies equally to L&D professionals themselves as it does to the clients they seek to serve.

STEP TWO: HIGH LEVEL DESIGN

Once you've got a sense of where you are, what you have, and what you are missing, you need to focus on the core elements needed to deliver your modern vision of OL&D. At the core of this focus lie three elements:

1. The strategic ethos you are adopting.
2. The story of where you are and where you want OL&D to be (and what this means for the wider organisation).
3. The data you prioritise, collect and analyse.

1. STRATEGIC ETHOS

Your strategic ethos must be underpinned by a desire to deliver services in a way that reflects the modern world. This is the distillation of everything we have looked at across CAPEX. In practical terms it will mean much of what you do will manifest itself a self-service model and real-time learning. There is no escape from this. Personalisation, technological development and a relentless focus on productivity, have dragged the self-service model to the fore.

You need to be able to align the experience you offer with experiences that have become standard in the consumer world. Take the banking industry, for example, where we can bank on the go in multiple different ways. We can go to an ATM, we can transfer money online, or we can use an app – whatever suits us best. Then we might go to a supermarket where we can choose to stand at a till or use self-service – and that is if we haven't ordered online already. After all that we might sit down to watch a movie streaming service where everything is ranked and categorised based on our preferences, and all available at the touch of a button.

All these examples seem so simple – ordinary even – but the changing expectations of consumers and customers mean learning functions must offer a similar service if they are to be taken seriously.

Your goal then is to offer a service and engage with people in such a way that they immerse themselves in learning as willingly as they do in other areas of their lives. Done well, this should never be a battle. We are naturally inquisitive. The vast reams of Google search data are an easy reminder of this. Google is seeing an average of 8.5bn searches every day. That is a massive daily quest for information. *Every single day.*[295]

Humans have a vast and unquenchable demand for learning. We just need to make sure we deliver it in a meaningful, engaging way by understanding what people want, how they want it and when they need it. You need to personalise, signpost and aggregate the content and provide nudges along the way so people continuously learn.

2. TELLING YOUR STORY

Every successful movement – and that is what you're trying to start – begins with a story about the future it is trying to build. It is then sustained by the stories that it generates off the back of this original narrative. This is understood by lots of companies, including Nike. There, all the top executive team members are 'designated corporate storytellers'.[296] Procter & Gamble went as far as bringing in Hollywood directors to teach its executives storytelling techniques.[297] It is unlikely you'll want to go quite as far as P&G, but Nike's approach is both relevant and attainable for you as a disciple of 21st Century OL&D. You need to be a storyteller and you need to persuade others to tell your story too.

To decide what that narrative should be, start with the goal you want to achieve. This requires you understand your audience(s) and their goals so you can ascribe value to what you are offering them. As such, you need to understand their motivations, their hopes, and their difficulties. You obviously can't talk to everyone at once as you start to shape your story. Instead, start by focusing on a core group of people who are passionate about your cause and who will be your ambassadors across the business. Talk to them; engage with them. Scott Goodson advocates gathering information that focuses on their 'interests, needs, goals, habits and issues'.[298] Once you've done this you can start to craft the right messages that align your goals with their desires, concerns and priorities.

Very often, when organisations begin to roll out change initiatives, the tendency is to present the facts, offering a data-driven business case for making the change. Facts are important. But it is how you use them in the context of storytelling that matters if you want to have maximum impact. Research indicates that our ability to recall a given fact is multiplied twentyfold if presented within a story.[299] Other research found a story is up to 22 times more memorable than facts alone. It is believed the sense of context that stories give is a key driver in the development of our memories from childhood onwards.[300]

Strong, impactful, emotive stories will only become more important as facts and data come at us in ever greater-volumes and at ever-greater speeds. We live in a world of information overload and message saturation. Our attention spans are getting shorter. Cutting through the noise and being heard is becoming harder and harder. Those who can tell an engaging story are the ones who will successfully communicate their important messages.

In the words of Leo Widrich, who paraphrases Princeton neuroscientist Uri Hasson, 'a story is the only way to activate parts in the brain so that a listener turns the story into their own idea and experience'.[301] What he's saying is we are hard-wired for stories to impact us and influence us. Stories engage the frontal and parietal cortices of your brain, which leads to a deeper sense of emotional engagement with what is happening (hence why you are so much more likely to remember a story with facts than just facts alone). Good stories can result in your brain releasing oxytocin, a hormone linked to empathy that is key to developing connections, as well as building and maintaining healthy relationships. As such, they make you better disposed towards the storyteller. Stories loaded with tension can lead to the stress hormone cortisol being released into your bloodstream. The hormone might be different but the result is the same: greater immersion in and responsiveness to the messages being imparted. Either way, you are making a powerful connection with your audience that will vastly improve their engagement with what you have to say.

Marshall Ganz, Senior Lecturer in Leadership, Organizing, and Civil Society at the Kennedy School of Government at Harvard University, is known for his work in mobilising social and political movements. Much of this work involves leveraging the power of narratives. Ganz believes:

Stories not only teach us how to act – they inspire us to act. Stories communicate our values through the language of the heart, our emotions. And it is what we feel – our hopes, our cares, our obligations – not simply what we know that can inspire us with the courage to act.[302]

If you get your storytelling right, it will become crucial in your transformation of OL&D. And that's just the start. By applying good storytelling to your learning output you can make OL&D a central resource in helping business to create, craft and tell stories that will inspire employees to act differently and behave differently, in turn equipping them to meet the challenges and opportunities heralded by the arrival of 4IR.

What then constitutes good storytelling? There are several key elements you must get right if you are going to cut through the content hurricane that batters employees from both outside and within an organisation.

Firstly – and most importantly – they need to be created for a defined audience. Ask yourself: can I answer the following questions…?

- Who am I talking to (and what is their relationship with me or the organisation I represent)?
- Where are they (both in terms of parts of the organisation and different geographies)?
- Why am I talking to them? (What problem are you solving for them?)
- What can I offer them that will solve that problem?
- How am I going to communicate with my audience?
- When should I talk to them?

Once you've established these and understand you audience, you can start crafting stories that are most likely to engage them. To do this effectively, stories need to contain as many of the core elements of good storytelling as possible. Marketing consultant, Michael Millar, defines these through the acronym TRUTH:

- Topical (i.e. of immediate relevance, interest, or importance due to current events)
- Relevant (to the audience you are addressing)
- Unusual (i.e. not something they've heard before or would expect, from you *or* from your industry/rivals)
- Tension (i.e. a sense that you are building to something or that there are important things at stake)
- Human (i.e. involving people and detailing the impact of your story on them).

He goes on to say you need to tell your story in a way that builds in as many of the following facets as possible:

- Relatability (telling the story in a way the audience can relate to)
- Novelty (it needs to be new and exciting to the audience)
- Fluency (the story must be told in a language they understand)
- Honesty/authenticity (the events or opinions are an accurate and fair reflection of the situation).

If you take these elements and use your knowledge of CAPEX to form a bond with your audience, you can leverage powerful business narratives, interwoven with data and facts, that will get the buy-in and support you need. Embedding these notions into the way the company communicates with its staff will quickly show measurable benefits, for example through improved employee satisfaction scores, lower turnover, and higher productivity.

3. TARGETING THE RIGHT DATA

The third core element you need consider in constructing your high-level programme design is the data you prioritise, collect and analyse. Technology and the data that it can generate are the cornerstones of 4IR and will be a key enabler of your success. But used wrongly, it can also make you drown. It is easy then to see data and analytics as very big and very scary, but the crucial thing to remember is they exist solely to:

- give you insight that aids decision-making
- offer concrete evidence of strategic necessity
- demonstrate return on investment for our activities.

If you collect data based on your understanding of your goals and how they can be measured, your audiences and what insights you need from them, as well as where technology can be brought to bear to have an impact, you will find yourself well-equipped to get executive buy-in and the investment needed to bring growth and transformation to your company.

That data will then become equally important in understanding how you are performing, what people need, and how that aligns with business KPIs. As you collect increased information you will be better equipped to focus on goal-orientated decision-making and to be a strategic partner in guiding your business as you see trends emerge.

Let us be clear: the return on investment that your data supports could be BIG. Research by consultants Accenture found that if companies could harness the full value of workforce data (while being careful to maintain high levels of employee trust), the 6,000 biggest publicly listed companies in the world alone stand to gain a combined value of three trillion dollars.[303]

And don't worry, you don't need to become a data scientist to make this work. This is all about understanding the purpose of collecting data (what is your goal?), knowing where to collect data from, and how to practically use data to gain insights. If you can start with a business need, you can work out what information you need to enable you to understand the current situation, and make the necessary decisions to succeed. So, we're talking about:

- **targeting** the data you need to make effective decisions (in as short a time as possible)
- **picking** and using data to build and shape relationships with relevant stakeholders in the context of what's important to the business
- **collecting**, analysing and presenting data in a way that allows people to make effective choices and decisions, as well as hold others to account.

Beware silos while you are doing this. The relevant data might not be at your fingertips. For instance, demographic data might sit in an HR system. Meanwhile, project and task related data might sit in a performance management system, while customer data will be with sales and marketing. This is all fine if you remember your goals, as they will dictate what you need to go and find to deliver.

The usefulness of workplace data is not restricted to internal teams. Regulators, shareholders, external partners, and investors are all interested in people data. Boards are now turning to frameworks like ISO 30414 – or 'Human Resource Management: Guidelines for Internal and External Human Capital Reporting' to give it its full title – as they consider their data and how to share it with external stakeholders.

The reason why ISO 30414 is where people are turning is because it is the first international standard that allows an organisation to get a clear view of the actual contribution of its human capital.[304]

Of course, data collection comes with important regulatory constraints, and ethical use of that data is paramount. However, even if you follow rules and regulations to the letter you must also make an extra effort to be transparent about your activities with staff. Employees want to know what data is collected on them and why. For example, sentiment analysis allows you to track keywords in emails and communications to monitor and improve engagement. However, that approach would be disastrous if, instead of facilitating engagement, it was seen as intrusive and created mistrust.

Employees will want to know how you and they each benefit from data collection and use. You need to be able to reassure them that that data is going to help their career or their experiences as an employee by better developing their skills and capabilities.

STEP THREE: STAKEHOLDER ENGAGEMENT

As you help prepare your organisation for the impact of 4IR, you will be asking a lot of people's time, resources, and expectations, as well as often challenging some deeply held beliefs. You will be looking at whole new ways of working and behaving. It is easy for such transformation projects – even with the right storytelling and early buy in – to lose momentum and go off the rails in the face of opposition, ambivalence or simple inertia. How then can we engage with our stakeholders to support and sustain these changes long enough to ensure they are embedded in the organisation's culture?

The first thing to do is step back and look at how other organisations have done it. Take solace from the fact you are not the first to try this and you will be far from the last. Once you've taken solace, take inspiration and ideas. This will help make it clear where it is best to invest your time, energy and talents.

You can start by revisiting the case studies throughout this book and taking advantage of the lessons that these pioneers spent their time and money learning. As we've said before, these firms may not be in your industry or even seem to bear any relevance to what you do, but they are there to be learnt from. The more companies you look to, the greater the collective intelligence you are tapping into. Early adopters of the CAPEX approach – for example, Santander, Unilever and FedEx Express – have positioned learning in a completely different way. Their work needs to be learnt from, built on and publicised to give people the belief and confidence they need to transform their own corner of L&D.

But don't just admire others from afar. Get in touch. Talk. Share ideas. Network. This is not something to fear. It is something that people relish. It is why so many of us are on sites like LinkedIn. Imagine what might come of these interactions, in terms of building relationships, gaining intelligence, joining the dots, and driving your agenda and performance. Better still, imagine what we could do if we created a sustained, inspiring movement based around the reinvention of the learning profession; a movement with positive behavioural and cultural change at its heart, and innovation and sustained success as its outcomes?

People and culture are bound together, each influencing and impacting the other. When it works at its best, learning is the glue that keeps those bonds sound and secure. Learning can be adaptable, flexible and durable. In bringing people and culture together, it embeds the right knowledge, attitudes and behaviours. So let us start that conversation among like-minded pioneers. Let us look at creating, building and maintaining a movement that isn't just restricted to your organisation, but helps drive the transformation of the whole learning profession. Let us join the fight for meaningful learning.

While this kind of external support and input will be very helpful in shaping your thinking and supporting you mentally, it is only by getting your stakeholders within your organisation on board that you will be able to start making change happen. That starts with getting a clear idea of who it is you need backing you. This is a matter of:

1. identifying all the people who are affected by your work, have influence over it, and who have an interest in its success of failure
2. prioritising them based on their interest in your work and the power they have over it
3. starting to understand them and what motivates them so you can shape your narrative in a way that appeals to them.

By the time you get into step three you'll be starting to get clarity and feedback on what good looks like from multiple perspectives in your organisation. You can then frame your offer – and hence your story – in the context of how learning activities will help solve their business problems.

These problems might be financially driven, the result of regulatory demands, a driver of the employer brand proposition, or any number of other things. The starting point is always to know what people care about. Don't be afraid to ask big, strategic questions of your key stakeholders, such as:

- What are their goals, vision and purpose?
- What do they believe are their CAPEX gaps?
- What are they worried about (now and in the future)?
- Who and what are their chief influencers?
- Where are they excelling?
- How can OL&D support them in any of these areas?
- What are their opinions on the current strengths, weaknesses and opportunities offered by learning, to both them and their teams?

Your company's leadership will of course, be core members of this key stakeholder group. Without their support you won't get far. They offer a great example of how to focus on Seth Godin's 'interests, needs, goals, habits and issues', which we mentioned a short time ago. We've tried to avoid that world-weary cliché that 'you need to speak the language of business' when we've spoken before about aligning your plans with the goals of the business. Nonetheless, that old cliché goes to the heart of how you understand, shape, sell, and deliver your activities. This language can be interpreted through the kind of questions senior leaders are asking modern, progressive learning teams to ensure their KPIs are focused on business outcomes. These are questions you need to be able to answer if you want to get influential early adopters on board. Once you've got a sense of their high-level needs, using the questions posed above, you can start drilling down deeper, by asking:

- What is the issue or problem we are seeking to remedy?
- What area(s) of performance are we looking to enhance?
- How does/will OL&D output deliver key business priorities?
- How do our activities link to increasing profit or help make more sales, faster?
- What can we do to enhance the customer or employee experience?
- How can we drive efficiencies in the operation and enhance profit margins?
- What impact are we having on our supply chain, and stock, goods and materials held?
- How do we align with, and deliver on the organisation's purpose, values and desired behaviour?
- Are we aligning the four levels of purpose with our people to harness their passions?
- How will our work impact the wellbeing, resilience and productivity of our people?
- How will we impact, improve and build the desired company culture?
- Are we harnessing the diversity of people?
- How are we impacting the employee and customer experience in and with our business?
- Are the skills for the future being developed in leaders at all levels of the organisation?
- How are we supporting collaboration and simplifying processes?
- How are you supporting and delivering the innovation our business needs for the future?

These are all solid, business-focused questions. If you can gather the relevant data to answer them you'll be well on the way to getting your story right and securing that crucial early buy-in. But, as we discussed above, be wary of forgetting to think about *how* you answer them. You might get away with telling a purely factual story when presenting your airtight business case for rolling out a CAPEX-based learning strategy, but you'll immediately falter when trying to garner the early (and, later, widespread) support you need if you can't weave an engaging story for your audience.

From the start, engaging with your stakeholders will require courageous conversations that you might normally shy away from. But it will be worth it. Undertaking this research will allow you to attain deeper insights, engagement, and understanding, and build a trust-based environment. It will let you connect learning to business goals and start building the data and the story that will get widespread buy-in. These insights will help hone the *purpose* of learning in your business and the direction organisational learning needs to go to drive your organisation on into 4IR. They will allow you to go back and reshape your strategic vision and to hone your story so that your stakeholders buy into your vision and continue to offer their support as you build your new learning paradigm.

As such, your strategy – and how you frame it through your story – will be born of an alignment of your goals with those of your business. But this is not enough. You also need to demonstrate how you will be accountable for these goals. If you can demonstrate where accountability lies it will make stakeholder engagement much easier. A word of caution: too often accountability can become a driver of fear that stifles creativity. This, in turn, reduces an organisation's ability to adapt and undermines the culture of trust that is fast becoming a core tenet of 4IR. The kind of accountability we are talking about is:

> *A personal choice to rise above one's circumstances and demonstrate the ownership necessary for achieving desired results – to See It, Own It, Solve It and Do It.*[305]

As you build your new approach to learning and take your stakeholders on a journey, you will need to develop, promote and embed a culture of accountability that goes beyond the traditional notion that only a single person can be accountable. You can instil the notion of joint accountability; where people share ownership for learning, decisions, actions and results. This is important because organisational results come from collective, not individual, activity. When an organisation fails to perform well it represents a collective or shared failure. When it performs well, you should be celebrating shared success. This joint accountability will begin when you start to engage with stakeholders and align your priorities with theirs.

Such joint accountability will serve you well as you proceed, as it will promote engagement in a positive organisational culture – a powerful driver of a collective sense of 'all being in it together'. For this reason, a complete understanding of accountability in organisations must include the principle of joint accountability. Once it is understood that everyone on the team and within the organisation is responsible for the culture and the organisation's purpose, the quicker we're able to hold everyone accountable for achieving the desired results, and the quicker we can build an organisational culture that survives and thrives.

STEP FOUR: START A MOVEMENT

We have now covered the key tenets of successful OL&D strategies and tactics in the age of 4IR. But getting widespread buy-in to your plans is something entirely different. We've looked at the 'language of business' – and that messaging is crucial in getting the ball rolling – as well as the keys to aligning your activities with key stakeholders and telling your story in a way that will maximise their buy-in. But systemic change requires ever-growing support and momentum. It requires you to engage with, and win over, an ever-growing number of people. In doing so you will ask them to give you some of their most precious things: their time, talent and energy. To do that, you need a movement.

On a Monday in August 2018, instead of attending her school lessons, a 15-year-old girl hand-painted a sign and cycled to the Swedish Parliament

– proceeding to sit outside it all day on 'strike'.[306] It was a relatively insignificant solo protest against the impact that we – as society – were having on our climate, but she vowed to repeat it until the Swedish government met its 2015 Paris Agreement carbon reduction commitments.[307] Within seven months, the 'Greta effect'[308] had grown beyond her wildest dreams, including inspiring similar protects in 2,233 locations on a single day, in an event that connected a million strikers across 128 countries.[309] Six months after that, *four million* protesters brought cities to a halt in 150 countries with 5,800 'events' across a week of global action.[310]

Before her first school strike, Greta Thunberg's greatest success in this arena had been winning a climate change essay competition.[311] By the end of 2018 – four months after she began protesting – she had won a place in *Time* magazine's list of the 25 'Most Influential' teenagers, and was one of its 100 'Most Influential' people just four months after that. Since then she has been awarded European Woman of the Year, won a place in the *Forbes* list of 100 'Most Powerful Women' (the youngest ever to do so), has been nominated for the Nobel Peace Prize more than once, and won multiple accolades.[312]

None of this could have happened at the rate and before the advent of 4IR. Digital technology now enables individuals and groups to connect, coordinate ideas and drive change in a manner unseen in human history. This deep-rooted connectivity means movements are springing up in ever-greater numbers as people feel either empowered by technology, or, conversely, struggle with isolation and fear about self-worth as a result feeling like a cog in a vast machine. These movements are springing up in greater numbers and growing at greater speeds than ever before. Compare the rapid – almost incidental – spread of Greta's movement to Nelson Mandela's struggle in the pre-digital age. In his book, *Long Walk to Freedom,* Mandela said 'when you start a movement, you must prepare for a long journey' and that progress 'is never a simple leap to your destination'.[313] How things have changed.

But the technology behind this trend must not be mistaken for a cause; it is merely the enabler. It is the nature of movements that are at the root of their attraction and their success. Movements offer purpose, meaning and fulfilment, whether they are a small, but locally important campaigns (such as stopping the local library closure, challenging a development, or raising funds for charity), or global phenomena like the #MeToo, #BeKind or Black Lives Matter movements.

What is fundamental is that we – as leaders – recognise the breathtaking pace, global impact and effectiveness of movements in harnessing people to drive change. Writing about the power of social movements, Harvard's Marshall Ganz says:

> *Social movements make a vital contribution to our capacity for economic, social, political, and cultural adaptation and renewal.*[314]

By replacing the word 'social' with 'organisational', Ganz's idea becomes all the more salient to the challenges around adaptation and renewal that businesses face today.

There is no reason why the movement that you start, whether it be to shape a positive culture, enable adaptability and innovation, promote a sense of purpose, or anything else, cannot offer meaning and fulfilment in the same way as any other movement. Moreover, a successful movement becomes self-fulfilling as it gathers momentum and cascades through an organisation.

Even if they seem organic, unplanned, or, on occasion almost magical in how they spread, movements that drive change do not just happen by accident. Professional services firm Deloitte identified five characteristics that are essential to creating and sustaining any movement. I have added some notes on why this is important, and how to achieve these:[315]

1. The corporation has a wider social purpose that resonates with people.
2. It aligns with people's core attitudes and beliefs, connecting like-minded followers. This enables it to become bigger than the individual instigating or encouraging involvement.

3. The organisation makes sincere and effective attempts to include those involved in the community, in whatever capacity that might be.
4. It must be associated with a clear reorganisation of society's values, conduct, or culture. This allows people to visibly display their commitment.
5. The movement must have a significant long-term effect on society. To do this, you will need to be authentic and transparent.

To start this momentum, you need to identify the people who are passionate about the cause, idea or innovation you are pushing. But before you approach them– let alone the wider organisation – you need to have something to tell them. You need to be able to clearly communicate the vision and the plan that incorporates all of Deloitte's points above, and which will form the basis of your movement. In other words, you need a story.

CREATING A MOVEMENT: AS EASY AS A–B–C

We have already looked at the underlying factors that drive a successful movement. Let us now look at the process you will need to go through to bring those factors to life. In his book *Cascades: How to Create a Movement that Drives Transformational Change* Greg Satell splits the process of creating a movement in three phases:[316]

A. the 'emergent phase' around the start of your movement
B. the 'engagement phase' around its growth
C. the 'success phase' when changes take root.

During all three phases you must remain focused on the long-term change you advocate. Satell sets out the following key principles:

- identify a pivotal change you want to make
- determine your vision and the difference you want to see and how a better future would look
- identify what you and your followers advocate
- describe the path to the key change and make the steps easy to follow (and make sure they're concrete and tangible)
- bring diverse groups of people together, including allies and organisational supporters.

FULLY COMMIT TO YOUR VALUES

Once you have established these building blocks, there are some key things you need to do to build and maintain momentum. Firstly, you need to be clear about your values and repeat your messages. This way your followers will understand and appreciate how your values align with theirs. It also gives everyone involved a framework for decision-making. This lets them know what is expected of them and how they should behave.

You then need to go about identifying and gathering the allies and supporters you need to build momentum. You should already have a core of allies through your stakeholder engagement efforts. Map out the different types of people who will support your idea, whether they be individuals with the right enthusiasm and commitment, leaders, networks, professional bodies or any other kinds of ambassador. What role will they play? Will they be active or passive supporters? Also think about the individuals or groups who form your opposition and how you can overcome this.

Once you are up and running you will need to gather small groups or teams who will amplify the movement across different networks. This is important because people will always seek 'social confirmation' before they embrace something new. As such, if you can establish small groups and teams to amplify your message and reach different kinds of people in different networks then it will go a long way to driving organisational change.

All the while, don't forget to listen to people. Too often people spreading their own message forget they need to listen to how it is being received. The more you can have conversations, the more everyone involved (or who you want to be involved) will be able to understand what each other wants and why. This will make the change more collaborative, familiar, acceptable, and even exiting. Conversely it will make it less scary.

As your movement takes off you've got to shout news of your successes from the rooftops. These stories not only make your movement more familiar and popular (and who doesn't want to be on the winning team?), they also give people the evidence they need to join or keep supporting the movement.

Once you've got people interested or involved, you've got to keep them on board by giving them a greater stake in the movement. Create opportunities for participation and connection that engage and empower your followers. If you are inclusive and allow people to actively take part, they will feel more aligned to your cause and a have a greater sense of ownership.

All the while remember the adage about 'best laid plans'. Adaptability is key. You will need to adapt your tactics as you go – maybe even your overarching strategy – as circumstances around you change. As long as the changes you make allow you to stay true to your values then the movement will continue to grow.

KEEP PUSHING UNTIL YOU REACH A TIPPING POINT

According to Malcolm Gladwell:

> *[A] tipping point is that magic moment when an idea, trend, or social behaviour crosses a threshold, tips, and spreads like wildfire.*[317]

This idea of a social tipping point applies equally to behaviour and standards in the workplace, or to any type of movement or initiative designed to change organisational culture. But when can you expect to reach that tipping point?

In *How Behavior Spreads*, Damon Centola examines how changes in societal behaviour occur – in areas such as voting, health, technology, and finance – and the ways social networks can be used to influence how they spread widely.[318]

Traditionally, it has been believed that more than half the population is required to effectuate significant social change.[319] Centola and his colleagues' research shows that when a quarter or more of the members of a given group are actively involved in social transformation, most of the others then rapidly acquiesce. Otherwise, the movement is doomed.[320]

On one occasion, just one individual determined the movement's ability to realise its dreams. They were the necessary key to bringing about that dramatic moment when something became the 'new normal'.[321] Even when the research team proactively incentivised people to not join the movement it only delayed the inevitable, raising the tipping point to 30%.

This all shows you don't need to think in terms of engaging your whole organisation, merely 25% of it. This makes it much easier to target and engage the groups you need to influence. After that the change you are seeking should come naturally. Once you've got 25% of people on board, it becomes more difficult for people to *not* join the movement.

When you get momentum behind you, be wary to not throw it away. Keep focused on the long-term change you advocate, and stay true to your values and purpose after early successes. This will ensure you make an enduring impact and instigate sustainable change. People must trust your motives and believe both you and your messages are authentic or they will quickly turn away. And remember, the movement ultimately needs to be about them, not you. The real heroes need to be the people making the change, not you.

A MANIFESTO FOR ORGANISATIONAL LEARNING & DEVELOPMENT

Can you – or will you – say this about your organisation's learning capacity?

- **Organisational learning and development has** a strategic purpose. It adds value. It shapes how an organisation behaves every day and enables transformational change by equipping colleagues to solve the increasingly broad and complex problems faced during the Fourth Industrial Revolution.
- **Organisational learning and development is** about cooperation and collaboration. It is independent, impartial and not tied to any special interests other than the triple bottom line of people, planet, and profit.
- **Organisational learning and development engages** in conversations and decisions that bring about positive change and are, at their heart, driven by the four levels of purpose (individual, team, organisational, and social) to ensure decisions are taken that steer the company forward in line with its vision and mission.
- **Organisational learning and development facilitates** and uses connected thinking across the business, bringing together people and culture and leadership, in order to shape the local, regional, industrial, societal, political and global agendas.

- **Organisational learning and development strives** in all its efforts to demonstrate entrepreneurship and creative leadership, while upholding the highest standards of governance.
- **Organisational learning and development provides** a service that reflects the wider consumer environment that employees are used to in their daily lives. These services take account of the organisational environment and individuals' needs so that they are engaging and inclusive.
- **Organisational learning and development shapes** and is shaped by a unique organisational culture. It believes that an organisation is accountable to all parts of society.
- **Organisational learning and development believes** that progress happens by bringing together people from all walks of life, to solve the complex problems an organisation faces, using their drive and influence to make positive change. It blends and balances the best of many kinds of thinking, from both the public and private sectors, international organisations and academic institutions.
- **Organisational learning and development relies** on data and analytics to improve decision-making processes, helping connect the right people with the right business intelligence. It will not shirk from having the difficult conversations this approach might demand, knowing that its expertise in – and support for – behavioural change, learning and development will enable people to collaborate and share knowledge, discover insights, and make the informed decisions needed to solve the complex problems that business and society face.
- **Organisational learning and development embraces** technology in a way that delivers real-time learning, aligning the practicalities of people's working lives with the individual passions, skills and experiences they need to develop to further the goals of business, as well as their careers.

- **Organisational learning and development will**, through all this activity, drive transformational change in the perception of learning, its strategic purpose, and its integration with the business.

If you can commit to these statements you are driving your business along the right path to the new world at work.

ENDNOTES

1 World Economic Forum, 'The Future of Jobs Report 2020' (Cologny, Switzerland: World Economic Forum, 20 October 2020), 48, https://www3.weforum.org/docs/WEF_Future_of_Jobs_2020.pdf

2 PwC, 'Talent Trends 2019: Upskilling for a Digital World', Annual Global CEO Survey Trends (London: PwC, 2019), 3, https://www.pwc.com/gx/en/ceo-survey/2019/Theme-assets/reports/talent-trends-report.pdf

3 IBM Institute for Business Value, 'Performance Data and Benchmarking 2018 Talent Development Survey' (Armonk, NY: IBM Institute for Business Value, 2018). Cited in LaPrade et al., 'The Enterprise Guide to Closing the Skills Gap', 6, https://www.ibm.com/downloads/cas/EPYMNBJA

4 Phillip Campbell, 'The Neuroscience of Adult Learning: a talk with Phillip Campbell', interview by Andrew Dyer, video and text interview, 2 April 2019, https://www.bcg.com/publications/2019/neuroscience-adult-learning-talk-with-phillip-campbell

5 Peter Hinssen, 'Peter Hinssen Wants You to Embrace the "Never Normal"', interview by Casey Gale, text interview, 23 December 2020, https://www.pcma.org/peter-hinssen-embrace-never-normal/

6 CIPD, 'Organisational development,' CIPD, https:// www.cipd.org/uk/knowledge/factsheets/organisational-development-factsheet/ (accessed 9 February 2021)

7 The Economist, 'The Importance of People People – the Coronavirus Crisis Thrusts Corporate HR Chiefs into the Spotlight', The Economist, 24 March 2020, https://www.cipd.org/uk/knowledge/factsheets/organisational-development-factsheet/

8 Henning Kagermann, Wolf-Dieter Lukas, and Wolfgang Wahlster, 'Industrie 4.0: Mit dem Internet der Dinge auf dem Weg zur 4. industriellen Revolution', ngenieur.de, 1 April 2011, https://www.ingenieur.de/technik/fachbereiche/produktion/industrie-40-mit-internet-dinge-weg-4-industriellen-revolution/

9 Klaus Schwab, 'The Fourth Industrial Revolution', Foreign Affairs, 12 December 2015, https://www.foreignaffairs.com/articles/2015-12-12/fourth-industrial-revolution

10 Nicholas Davis, 'What Is the Fourth Industrial Revolution?', World Economic Forum (blog), 19 January 2016, https://www.weforum.org/agenda/2016/01/what-is-the-fourth-industrial-revolution/

11 Klaus Schwab, 'The Fourth Industrial Revolution: What It Means, How to Respond', World Economic Forum (blog), 14 January 2016, https://www.weforum.org/agenda/2016/01/the-fourth-industrial-revolution-what-it-means-and-how-to-respond/

12 Gerd Leonhard, Technology vs. Humanity: The Coming Clash Between Man and Machine (Zurich: The Futures Agency, 2016)

13 James Manyika et al., 'Harnessing Automation for a Future That Works' (New York: McKinsey Global Institute, 12 January 2017), 5, https://www.mckinsey.com/~/media/McKinsey/Featured%20Insights/Digital%20Disruption/Harnessing%20automation%20for%20a%20future%20that%20works/MGI-A-future-that-works_Full-report.pdf

14 World Economic Forum, 'Future of Work', World Economic Forum, https://www.weforum.org/projects/future-of-work (accessed 9 February 2021)

15 Roland Berger, 'Think Act: Beyond Mainstream – the Industrie 4.0 Transition Quantified. How the Fourth Industrial Revolution Is Reshuffling the Economic, Social and Industrial Model' (Munich: Roland Berger), 15, https://www.rolandberger.com/en/Insights/Publications/The-Industrie-4.0-transition-quantified.html (accessed 9 February 2021)

16 'Press Conference – Australian Parliament House Act', Prime Minister of Australia, 29 March 2020, https://pmtranscripts.pmc.gov.au/release/transcript-42764

17 Office for National Statistics, 'UK Whole Economy: Output per Hour Worked % Change per Annum SA', Office for National Statistics, 19 January 2021, https://www.ons.gov.uk/employmentandlabourmarket/peopleinwork/labourproductivity/timeseries/lzvd/prdy; Royal Statistical Society, 'RSS Announces Statistics of the Decade', Royal Statistical Society (blog), 23 December 2019, https://rss.org.uk/news-publication/news-publications/2019/general-news-(1)/rss-announces-statistics-of-the-decade/

18 The Prince's Trust, 'The Prince's Trust eBay Youth Index 2019' (London: The Prince's Trust, 2019), 7, https://www.princes-trust.org.uk/about-the-trust/news-views/ebay-youth-index-2019

19 Laura Overton and Genny Dixon, 'Preparing for the Future of Learning: A Changing Perspective for L&D Leaders', In-Focus Report (London: CIPD, April 2016), 16, https://www.cipd.co.uk/Images/preparing-for-the-future-of-learning_2016-a-changing-perspective-for-l-and-d-leaders_tcm18-13846.pdf

20 Daly and Ahmetaj, 'Back to the Future: Why Tomorrow's Workforce Needs a Learning Culture', 41.

21 LinkedIn Learning, '2017 Workplace Learning Report' (Sunnyvale, CA: LinkedIn), 12, https://learning.linkedin.com/content/dam/me/learning/en-us/pdfs/lil-workplace-learning-report.pdf (accessed 9 Feburary 2021)

22 Deloitte, 'Deloitte Millennial Survey 2018: Millennials Disappointed in Business, Unprepared for Industry 4.0' (London: Deloitte, 2018), 23, https://www2.deloitte.com/tr/en/pages/about-deloitte/articles/millennialsurvey-2018.html
23 Mary Baker, 'Motivate Employees to Reskill for the Digital Age', Gartner (blog), 18 March 2019, https://www.gartner.com/smarterwithgartner/motivate-employees-to-reskill-for-the-digital-age/
24 Cathryn Newberry, 'The More Digitised We Are, the More Human We Become', CIPHR (blog), 11 June 2019, https://www.ciphr.com/news/leena-nair-cogx/
25 Gerald F. Seib, 'In Crisis, Opportunity for Obama', The Wall Street Journal, 21 November 2008, sec. U.S., https://www.wsj.com/articles/SB122721278056345271
26 Josh Bersin, 'A New Paradigm for Corporate Training: Learning in the Flow of Work', Josh Bersin (blog), 3 June 2018, https://joshbersin.com/2018/06/a-new-paradigm-for-corporate-training-learning-in-the-flow-of-work/
27 Ibid.
28 David Green, 'Making Learning a Habit That Matters at Ericsson', LinkedIn (blog), 13 October 2020, https://www.linkedin.com/pulse/making-learning-habit-matters-ericsson-david-green
29 David Kelleher, 'Survey: 81% of U.S. Employees Check Their Work Mail Outside Work Hours [INFOGRAPHIC]', TechTalk: Powered by GFI Software (blog), 20 May 2013, https://techtalk.gfi.com/survey-81-of-u-s-employees-check-their-work-mail-outside-work-hours/
30 Annette Sinclair, 'Health and Well-Being at Work' (London: CIPD, May 2018), 3, https://www.cipd.co.uk/Images/health-and-well-being-at-work_tcm18-40863.pdf
31 John F. Helliwell et al., eds, '2020 World Happiness Report' (New York: Sustainable Development Solutions Network, 2020), 25, https://worldhappiness.report/ed/2020/
32 Ian Hesketh and Cary L. Cooper, 'Leaveism at Work', Occupational Medicine 64, no. 3 (1 April 2014): 146, https://doi.org/10.1093/occmed/kqu025
33 Ibid.
34 The American Institute of Stress, 'Workplace Stress', The American Institute of Stress, https://www.stress.org/wp-content/uploads/2011/08/2001Attitude-in-the-Workplace-Harris.pdf (accessed 10 February 2021)
35 Eastern Kentucky University, 'Work Related Stress on Employees Health', EKU Online (blog), https://safetymanagement.eku.edu/blog/work-related-stress-on-employees-health/ (accessed 10 February 2021)
36 Jeffrey Pfeffer, Dying for a Paycheck: How Modern Management Harms Employee Health and Company Performance – and What We Can Do About It (New York: Harper Business, 2018).
37 Newberry, 'The More Digitised We Are, the More Human We Become'.

38 Ashleigh Webber, 'Why, for Unilever, Wellbeing Has to Start with Local Culture Change', Personnel Today, 4 December 2020, https://www.personneltoday.com/hr/why-for-unilever-wellbeing-has-to-start-with-local-culture-change/
39 Ibid.
40 Derek Mowbray, 'The Wellbeing and Performance Agenda: Making the Workplace a Fabulous and High Performing Place to Work' (Cheltenham, UK: Management Advisory Service, December 2016), 10, https://www.mas.org.uk/uploads/artlib/wellbeing-and-performance-agenda-2016.pdf
41 Ibid.
42 Seth Godin, Tribes: We Need You to Lead Us (London: Piatkus, 2014).
43 Professor Barbara Fredrickson, Positivity.
44 Richard Wiseman, 59 Seconds: Think a Little, Change a Lot (London: Pan Books, 2009).
45 Shawn Achor, The Happiness Advantage: The Seven Principles That Fuel Success and Performance at Work (London: Virgin Books, 2011).
46 David R. Hamilton, 'Did You Know You're a Chemist?', David R Hamilton PhD (blog), 21 October 2013, https://drdavidhamilton.com/did-you-know-youre-a-chemist/
47 Neel Doshi and Lindsay McGregor, Primed to Perform: How to Build the Highest Performing Cultures through the Science of Total Motivation (New York: Harper Business, 2015)
48 Clement Bellet, Jan-Emmanuel De Neve, and George Ward, 'Does Employee Happiness Have an Impact on Productivity?', Saïd Business School WP 2019-13, 10 November 2020, 25, https://doi.org/10.2139/ssrn.3470734
49 University of Oxford, 'Happy Workers Are 13% More Productive', University of Oxford (blog), 24 October 2019, https://www.ox.ac.uk/news/2019-10-24-happy-workers-are-13-more-productive
50 Helliwell et al., eds, '2020 World Happiness Report', 31.
51 Ibid.
52 Tony Hsieh, 'How I Did It: Tony Hsieh, CEO, Zappos.com', Inc., 1 September 2006, https://www.inc.com/magazine/20060901/hidi-hsieh.html
53 Aarti Venkatraman, 'The Moving Parts of Amazon and Jeff Bezos' Empire', Inc42, 22 June 2017, https://inc42.com/buzz/amazon-jeff-bezos-empire/
54 D. D. Warrick, John F. Milliman, and Jeffery M. Ferguson, 'Building High Performance Cultures', Organizational Dynamics, 45, no. 1 (January 2016): 64, https://doi.org/10.1016/j.orgdyn.2015.12.008
55 D. D. Warrick, John F. Milliman, and Jeffery M. Ferguson, 'Building High Performance Cultures', Organizational Dynamics, 45, no. 1 (January 2016): 64–70, https://doi.org/10.1016/j.orgdyn.2015.12.008
56 Ibid., 4–5.
57 Ibid., 5.

58 Ibid.
59 Tony Hsieh, Delivering Happiness: A Path to Profits, Passion, and Purpose (New York: Business Plus, 2011).
60 Warrick, Milliman, and Ferguson, 'Building High Performance Cultures', 4.
61 Edelman Trust Barometer https://www.edelman.com/trust/trust-barometer (accessed 9 May 2022)
62 Rita Watson, 'Oxytocin: The Love and Trust Hormone Can Be Deceptive', Psychology Today, 14 October 2013, https://www.psychologytoday.com/gb/blog/love-and-gratitude/201310/oxytocin-the-love-and-trust-hormone-can-be-deceptive
63 Paul J. Zak, 'The Neuroscience of Trust', Harvard Business Review, January–February 2017, https://hbr.org/2017/01/the-neuroscience-of-trust
64 Stephen M. R. Covey with Rebecca R. Merrill, The Speed of Trust: The One Thing That Changes Everything (New York: Free Press, 2008).
65 John Lewis Partnership, 'Our Values', John Lewis Partnership, https://www.johnlewispartnership.co.uk/about/our-values.html (accessed 11 February 2021); John Spedan Lewis, Partnership for All: A Thirty Four Year Old Experiment in Industrial Democracy (London: Kerr-Cross Publishing, 1948), cover, 64. Cited in Abigail Cathcart, 'Directing Democracy: The Case of the John Lewis Partnership' (Doctoral thesis, Leicester, UK, University of Leicester, 2009), 4, 14, https://eprints.qut.edu.au/44149/
66 John Lewis Partnership, 'Our Values'.
67 Zoe Wood, 'The John Lewis Model and What Others Could Learn from It', The Guardian, 16 January 2012, sec. Business, https://www.theguardian.com/business/2012/jan/16/john-lewis-model-lessons.
68 John Lewis Partnership, 'How We Share Power', John Lewis Partnership, https://www.johnlewispartnership.co.uk/about/how-we-share-power.html (accessed 11 February 2021)
69 Claire Hastwell, 'The Business Returns on High-Trust Work Culture', Great Place to Work (blog), 12 September 2019, https://www.greatplacetowork.com/resources/blog/the-business-returns-on-high-trust-work-culture
70 Zak, 'The Neuroscience of Trust'.
71 Hastwell, 'The Business Returns on High-Trust Work Culture'.
72 Zak, 'The Neuroscience of Trust'.
73 Great Place to Work, 'Connecting People and Purpose: 7 Ways High-Trust Organizations Retain Talent – Findings from the 2016 Fortune 100 Best Companies to Work For®' (Oakland, CA: Great Place to Work), https://learn.greatplacetowork.com/rs/520-AOO-982/ images/GPTW-Fortune-100Best-Report-2016.pdf (accessed 11 February 2021)
74 Great Place to Work research High-trust cultures.
75 The Neuroscience of Trust (HBR) by Paul J. Zak.
76 Schwab, 'The Fourth Industrial Revolution: What It Means, How to Respond'.

77 Plato, 'Cratylus', 402a, in Plato in Twelve Volumes, trans. Harold N. Fowler, vol. 12, 12 vols (Cambridge, MA: Harvard University Press, 1921), http://data.perseus.org/citations/urn:cts:greekLit:tlg0059.tlg005.perseus-eng1:402a While there is much controversy over the legitimacy of this quotation as part of Heraclitus' worldview, this is not relevant for our purposes. See David G. Stern, 'Heraclitus' and Wittgenstein's River Images: Stepping Twice into the Same River', The Monist 74, no. 4 (1991): 579–81.
78 Avil Beckford, 'You Cannot Step into the Same River Twice', The Invisible Mentor (blog), 5 April 2020, https://theinvisiblementor.com/you-cannot-step-into-the-same-river-twice/
79 Josh Bersin, 'Responding to COVID-19. Ten Lessons from the World's HR Leaders', Josh Bersin (blog), 1 April 2020, https://joshbersin.com/2020/04/responding-to-covid-19-ten-lessons-from-the-worlds-hr-leaders/
80 Simon Brown, Episode 44: How Novartis Promotes Learning Curiosity to Drive Business Value (Interview with Simon Brown), interview by David Green, audio and text interview, 6 October 2020, https://www.myhrfuture.com/digital-hr-leaders-podcast/2020/10/6/how-novartis-promotes-learning-curiosity-to-drive-business-value
81 Henrik Kniberg and Anders Ivarsson, 'Scaling Agile @ Spotify with Tribes, Squads, Chapters & Guilds' (Stockholm: Crisp, October 2012), 2, 4, https://blog.crisp.se/wp-content/uploads/2012/11/SpotifyScaling.pdf
82 Ibid.
83 Joost, 'The World's Most Pioneering Company of Our Times', Corporate Rebels (blog), https://corporate-rebels.com/haier (accessed 11 February 2021)
84 Ibid.
85 Ibid.
86 Pfizer, 'Pfizer Forms Global Strategic Alliance with Merck Kgaa, Germany, to Jointly Develop and Commercialize Anti-PD-L1 to Accelerate Presence in Immuno-Oncology', Pfizer (blog), 16 November 2014, https://www.pfizer.com/news/press-release/press-release-detail/pfizer_forms_global_strategic_alliance_with_merck_kgaa_germany_to_jointly_develop_and_commercialize_anti_pd_l1_to_accelerate_presence_in_immuno_oncology
87 Zoe Kleinman, 'Uber and Spotify Launch Car Music Playlist Partnership', BBC News, 17 November 2014, sec. Tech, https://www.bbc.co.uk/news/technology-30080974
88 GoPro, 'GoPro and Red Bull Form Exclusive Global Partnership', GoPro (blog), 23 May 2016, https://gopro.com/en/us/news/gopro-and-red-bull-form-exclusive-global-partnership
89 Henry Farrell, 'Diversity Isn't Just about Justice. It's about Helping Us Make Better Collective Decisions.', The Washington Post, 28 September 2017, sec. Monkey Cage, https://www.washingtonpost.com/news/monkey-cage/wp/2017/09/28/diversity-isnt-just-about-justice-its-about-helping-us-make-better-collective-decisions/

90 Yves Morieux and Peter Tollman, Six Simple Rules: How to Manage Complexity without Getting Complicated (Brighton, MA: Harvard Business Review Press, 2014).
91 Boston Consulting Group, 'To Cope with Complexity, Leaders Must Learn What Employees Actually Do; Usual Management Toolkits Are Likely Counter-Productive, Says New Book by The Boston Consulting Group', Boston Consulting Group (blog), 7 April 2014, https://www.bcg.com/en-gb/press/7april2014-cope-with-complexity-leaders-learn-what-employees-do
92 Jacques Bughin et al., 'Skill Shift: Automation and the Future of the Workforce', discussion paper (New York: McKinsey Global Institute, 2018), https://www.mckinsey.com/featured-insights/future-of-work/skill-shift-automation-and-the-future-of-the-workforce
93 Joseph Pistrui, 'The Future of Human Work Is Imagination, Creativity, and Strategy', Harvard Business Review, 18 January 2018, https://hbr.org/2018/01/the-future-of-human-work-is-imagination-creativity-and-strategy
94 Jeff Schwartz, Heather Stockton, and Kelly Monahan, 'Forces of Change: The Future of Work', A Deloitte Series on Future of Work (London: Deloitte, 9 November 2017), https://www2.deloitte.com/us/en/insights/focus/technology-and-the-future-of-work/overview.html
95 World Economic Forum, 'The Future of Jobs Report 2018' (Cologny, Switzerland: World Economic Forum, 17 September 2018), https://www.weforum.org/reports/the-future-of-jobs-report-2018
96 James P. Spillane, Distributed Leadership, The Jossey-Bass Leadership Library in Education (San Francisco: Jossey-Bass, 2006).
97 Jon Ingham, The Social Organization: Developing Employee Connections and Relationships for Improved Business Performance (New York: Kogan Page, 2017).
98 Jack Zenger, 'We Wait Too Long to Train Our Leaders', Harvard Business Review, 17 December 2012, https://hbr.org/2012/12/why-do-we-wait-so-long-to-trai
99 Nuffield Trust, 'The NHS Is the World's Fifth Largest Employer' (Nuffield Trust, 27 October 2017), https://www.nuffieldtrust.org.uk/chart/the-nhs-is-the-world-s-fifth-largest-employer
100 Ibid.
101 NHS, 'Results from Northamptonshire Healthcare NHS Foundation Trust', 2016 National NHS Staff Survey (London: National Health Service), https://www.nhsstaffsurveys.com/Caches/Files/NHS_staff_survey_2016_RP1_full.pdf (accessed 11 February 2021)
102 Care Quality Commission, 'Northamptonshire Healthcare NHS Foundation Trust: Quality Report' (London: Quality Care Commission, 26 August 2015), https://api.cqc.org.uk/public/v1/reports/3ab3e30f-b199-4f79-b532-d0bce6317330?20210127060845

103 Care Quality Commission, 'Northamptonshire Healthcare NHS Foundation Trust: Inspection Report' (London: Quality Care Commission, 16 August 2018), https://api.cqc.org.uk/public/v1/reports/d77d9664-8545-499f-b27e-2519b3e2c458?20210117144847
104 Northamptonshire Healthcare NHS Foundation Trust, 'Annual Reports & Accounts 2015/16' (Kettering, UK: Northamptonshire Healthcare NHS Foundation Trust, 2016), 31, https://www.nhft.nhs.uk/download.cfm?doc=docm93jijm4n5139.pdf&ver=14727
105 Northamptonshire Healthcare NHS Foundation Trust, 'Annual Reports & Accounts 2018/19' (Kettering, UK: Northamptonshire Healthcare NHS Foundation Trust, 2019), 36, https://www.nhft.nhs.uk/download.cfm?doc=docm93jijm4n13215.pdf&ver=31407
106 The Lego Playground: https://www.youtube.com/watch?v=X_UlCRPnAtI
107 Leadership at the Lego Group https://www.youtube.com/watch?v=J90R6jWm2gA
108 Oliver Bussmann, 'On the Global Workforce', in 'The World in 2033: Big Thinkers and Futurists Share Their Thoughts', ed. Todd Wilms, Forbes, 8 February 2013, https://www.forbes.com/sites/sap/2013/02/08/the-world-in-2033-big-thinkers-and-futurists-share-their-thoughts/?sh=3dcea6405205
109 Ibid.
110 PwC, 'Workforce of the Future: The Competing Forces Shaping 2030' (London: PwC, 2018), 8, https://www.pwc.com/talent-trends-ceo-survey/.
111 Celeste Campbell, 'What Is Neuroplasticity?', BrainLine (blog), https://www.brainline.org/author/celeste-campbell/qa/whatneuroplasticity (accessed 12 February 2021)
112 The Growth Mindset, Dr Carol Dweck, 2015.
113 Gerry Vassar, 'Neuroplasticity: Hope for Changing Your Brain', Lakeside Educational Network (blog), 20 November 2014, https://lakesidelink.com/blog/lakeside/neuroplasticity-hope-for-changing-your-brain/
114 Ibid; Fit4D, 'The Neuroscience of Behavior Change', StartUp Health, 8 August 2017, https://healthtransformer.co/the-neuroscience-of-behavior-change-bcb567fa83c1
115 William James, Habit, (Whitefish, MT: Kessinger Publishing, 2003).
116 Kelly McGonigal, The Willpower Instinct: How Self-Control Works, Why It Matters, and What You Can Do to Get More of It (New York: Avery Publishing Group, 2013).
117 Shawn Achor, The Happiness Advantage: The Seven Principles That Fuel Success and Performance at Work (London: Virgin Books, 2011).
118 Josh Kaufman, The First 20 Hours: How to Learn Anything Fast (New York: Portfolio Penguin, 2013).
119 K. Anders Ericsson, Michael J. Prietula, and Edward T. Cokely, 'The Making of an Expert', Harvard Business Review, 2007, https://hbr.org/2007/07/the-making-of-an-expert.

120 James Clear, 'How Long Does It Actually Take to Form a New Habit? (Backed by Science)', James Clear (blog),https://jamesclear.com/new-habit (accesssed 16 February 2021)
121 Ibid.
122 Phillippa Lally et al., 'How Are Habits Formed: Modelling Habit Formation in the Real World', European Journal of Social Psychology 40, no. 6 (16 July 2009): 1007, https://doi.org/10.1002/ejsp.674
123 Ibid.
124 Bersin, 'A New Paradigm for Corporate Training: Learning in the Flow of Work.'
125 Harvard Business Review, 'The Business Case for Purpose', Harvard Business Review Analytic Services Report (Brighton, MA: Harvard Business Review), 1, https://hbr.org/resources/pdfs/comm/ey/19392HBRReportEY.pdf (accessed 16 February 2021)
126 Datamaran, 'Materiality Definition: The Ultimate Guide', Datamaran, https://www.datamaran.com/materiality-definition/ (accessed 16 February 2021)
127 See MSCI, 'ESG Ratings: Measuring a Company's Resilience to Long-Term, Financially Relevant ESG Risks', MSCI, https://www.msci.com/our-solutions/esg-investing/esg-ratings (accessed 16 February 2021)
128 Thomas W. Malnight, Ivy Buche, and Charles Dhanaraj, 'Put Purpose at the Core of Your Strategy', Harvard Business Review, October 2019, https://hbr.org/2019/09/put-purpose-at-the-core-of-your-strategy
129 Ibid.
130 Ibid.
131 Malnight, Buche, and Dhanaraj, 'Put Purpose at the Core of Your Strategy'.
132 Simon Sinek, 'How Great Leaders Inspire Action' (TEDx talk, TEDxPugetSound, Newcastle, WA, 16 September 2009), https://www.ted.com/talks/simon_sinek_how_great_leaders_inspire_action. Simon makes this statement at c. 4:26.
133 Eric Garton and Michael Mankins, 'Engaging Your Employees Is Good, but Don't Stop There', Harvard Business Review, 9 December 2015, https://hbr.org/2015/12/engaging-your-employees-is-good-but-dont-stop-there
134 Ibid.
135 Cathy Carlisi et al., 'Purpose with the Power to Transform Your Organization' (Boston, MA: Boston Consulting Group, 15 May 2017), https://www.bcg.com/publications/2017/transformation-behavior-culture-purpose-power-transform-organization
136 LinkedIn Talent Solutions, '2020 Global Talent Trends: 4 Trends Changing the Way You Attract and Retain Talent' (Sunnyvale, CA: LinkedIn, 2020), 13, https://business.linkedin.com/content/dam/me/business/en-us/talent-solutions/resources/pdfs/linkedin-2020-global-talent-trends-report.pdf
137 Simon Lowe et al., 'Corporate Governance Review 2019' (London: Grant Thornton, 2019), 12, https://www.grantthornton.co.uk/

globalassets/1.-member-firms/united-kingdom/pdf/publication/2019/corporate-governance-review-2019.pdf
138 Unilever, 'Our Strategy for Sustainable Growth', Unilever, https://www.unilever.com/sustainable-living/our-strategy/ (accessed 17 February 2021)
139 Unilever, 'Our Strategy', Unilever, https://www.unilever.com/about/who-we-are/our-strategy/ (accessed 17 February 2021)
140 Unilever, 'Top Sustainability Index Awards Unilever Industry Leader in Personal Products', Unilever (blog), 17 November 2020, https://www.unilever.com/news/news-and-features/Feature-article/2020/top-sustainability-index-awards-unilever-industry-leader-in-personal-products.html
141 Keith Ferrazzi, 'How Agile Is Helping Unilever Go Forward Faster', Forbes, 17 June 2020, https://www.forbes.com/sites/keithferrazzi/2020/06/17/how-agile-is-helping-unilever-go-forward-faster/?sh=3306e0221020
142 Unilever, 'Unilever Achieves Gender Balance across Management Globally', Unilever (blog), 3 March 2020, https://www.unilever.com/news/press-releases/2020/unilever-achieves-gender-balance-across-management-globally.html
143 See e.g., Sofi Jaku, 'Unilever's Success Story: Wake up Call for English Proficiency', EF – Education First (blog), https://www.ef.com/wwen/blog/corporate/unilever-english-proficiency/ (accessed 17 February 2021).
144 Glassdoor, 'Unilever Reviews', Glassdoor, 14 February 2021, https://www.glassdoor.co.uk/Reviews/Unilever-Reviews-E3513.htm?filter.iso3Language=eng. Based on percentage who would 'Recommend to a Friend'. Data as of Glassdoor's 14 February 2021 update.
145 Alan Jope and Graeme Pitkethly, 'Unilever Full Year 2020: Results & Strategic Refresh' (London: Unilever, 4 February 2021), 35, https://www.unilever.com/Images/unilever-q4--and-full-year-2020-results-presentation_tcm244-558978_1_en.pdf
146 Unilever, 'Purpose-Led, Future-Fit: Unilever Annual Report and Accounts 2019' (London: Unilever, 2019), 6, https://www.unilever.com/investor-relations/annual-report-and-accounts/
147 Unilever, 'Unilever's Purpose-Led Brands Outperform', Unilever (blog), 11 June 2019, https://www.unilever.com/news/press-releases/2019/unilevers-purpose-led-brands-outperform.html
148 Ibid.
149 Jeff Fromm, 'Purpose Series: A Purpose-Driven Brand Is a Successful Brand', Forbes, 16 January 2019, https://www.forbes.com/sites/jefffromm/2019/01/16/purpose-series-a-purpose-driven-brand-is-a-successful-brand/?sh=64145e44437d
150 Larry Fink, 'Larry Fink's 2020 Letter to CEOs: A Fundamental Reshaping of Finance', 2020, https://www.blackrock.com/corporate/investor-relations/2020-larry-fink-ceo-letter

151 Ibid.
152 Ibid.
153 José Viñals, 'Here for Good Means Saying No to Coal', Standard Chartered (blog), 25 September 2018, https://www.sc.com/en/explore-our-world/here-for-good-means-saying-no-to-coal/
154 Standard Chartered, 'Extractive Industries', Standard Chartered, https://www.sc.com/en/sustainability/position-statements/extractive-industries/ (accessed 18 February 2021)
155 Amir Amel-Zadeh and George Serafeim, 'Why and How Investors Use ESG Information: Evidence from a Global Survey', Financial Analysts Journal 74, no. 3 (2018): 30, https://doi.org/10.2139/ssrn.2925310
156 KPMG, 'Agile or Irrelevant: Redefining Resilience', Global CEO Outlook (London: KPMG International, 2019), 7, https://assets.kpmg/content/dam/kpmg/xx/pdf/2019/05/kpmg-global-ceo-outlook-2019.pdf
157 KPMG, 'Agile or Irrelevant', 7.
158 KPMG, 'Disrupt and Grow', Global CEO Outlook (London: KPMG International, 2017), 16, https://home.kpmg/content/dam/kpmg/uk/pdf/2017/06/2017-ceo-outlook.pdf
159 Michael Dimock, 'Defining Generations: Where Millennials End and Generation Z Begins', Pew Research Center Fact Tank (blog), 17 January 2019, https://www.pewresearch.org/fact-tank/2019/01/17/where-millennials-end-and-generation-z-begins/
160 Deloitte, 'The Deloitte Millennial Survey 2019: Societal Discord and Technological Transformation Create a "Generation Disrupted"' (London: Deloitte, 2019), 11, https://www2.deloitte.com/content/dam/Deloitte/global/Documents/About-Deloitte/deloitte-2019-millennial-survey.pdf
161 Edelman, 'Edelman Trust Barometer 2021' (Chicago: Edelman, 2021), 34, https://www.edelman.com/trust/2021-trust-barometer
162 Ibid., 35.
163 Survey for Futerra by OnePulse, November 2018. Quoted in Solitaire Townsend, '88% of Consumers Want You to Help Them Make a Difference', Forbes, 21 November 2018, https://www.forbes.com/sites/solitairetownsend/2018/11/21/consumers-want-you-to-help-them-make-a-difference/
164 Waitrose, 'Food and Drink Report 2018–19: The Era of the Mindful Consumer' (Bracknell, UK: Waitrose), 4, https://www.waitrose.com/content/dam/waitrose/Inspiration/Waitrose%20&%20 Partners%20Food%20and%20Drink%20Report%202018.pdf (accessed 18 February 2021)
165 Ibid.
166 Ibid.
167 Viktor E. Frankl, Man's Search for Meaning: The Classic Tribute to Hope from the Holocaust, trans. Ilse Lasch (London: Rider, 2004 [1946]).

168 Héctor García and Francesc Miralles, Ikigai: The Japanese Secret to a Long and Happy Life, trans. Heather Cleary (London: Hutchinson, 2017).

169 David Rock, 'SCARF®: A Brain-Based Model for Collaborating with and Influencing Others', NeuroLeadership Journal, no. 1 (2008), https://membership.neuroleadership.com/material/scarf-a-brain-based-model-for-collaborating-with-and-influencing-others-vol-1/

170 Team Tony, 'Do You Need to Feel Significant?', Tony Robbins (blog), https://www.tonyrobbins.com/mind-meaning/do-you-need-to-feel-significant/ (accessed 18 February 2021)

171 Susan Cain, Quiet: The Power of Introverts in a World That Can't Stop Talking (London: Penguin Books, 2013).

172 Ibid.

173 Internal letter reproduced publicly by author as Satya Nadella, 'Coming Together to Combat COVID-19', LinkedIn (blog), 21 March 2020, https://www.linkedin.com/pulse/coming-together-combat-covid-19-satya-nadella/

174 Amy Wrzesniewski et al., 'Jobs, Careers, and Callings: People's Relations to Their Work', Journal of Research in Personality 31, no. 1 (March 1997): 25, https://doi.org/10.1006/jrpe.1997.2162

175 Patrick L. Hill et al., 'Sense of Purpose Moderates the Associations Between Daily Stressors and Daily Well-Being', Annals of Behavioral Medicine 52, no. 8 (13 July 2018): 726–29, https://doi.org/10.1093/abm/kax039. Thank you to Cornell University's Bronfenbrenner Center for Translational Research (BCTR), whose article in Psychology Today made me aware of Anthony Burrow, as well as this study, and the one cited in the next footnote. See BCTR, '"Knowing Your Why" Is Good for You', Psychology Today, 24 June 2019, https://www.psychologytoday.com/gb/blog/evidence-based-living/201906/knowing-your-why-is-good-you

176 Dan Witters, '10 Ways Leaders Can Improve Engagement and Wellbeing', Gallup (blog), 6 October 2020, https://www.gallup.com/workplace/320108/ways-leaders-improve-engagement-wellbeing.aspx

177 Patrick L. Hill et al., 'The Value of a Purposeful Life: Sense of Purpose Predicts Greater Income and Net Worth', Journal of Research in Personality 65 (December 2016): 40, https://doi.org/10.1016/j.jrp.2016.07.003

178 While this quote is often attributed to Mark Twain, William Barclay and others, per Quote Investigator, there is presently insufficient evidence to permit this. See Quote Investigator, 'Two Most Important Days in Your Life: The Day You Were Born and the Day You Discover Why', Quote Investigator, 25 May 2017, https://quoteinvestigator.com/2016/06/22/why/

179 See e.g., Simon Sinek, Nested WHYs, YouTube video, 8 November 2017, https://www.youtube.com/watch?v=uCOGZoME4ro

180 Mark Truelson, 'Defining Your Team's Purpose', Mark Truelson (blog), November 2017, http://marktruelson.com/defining-your-teams-purpose/

181 Clive Gilson et al., Peak Performance: Inspirational Business Lessons from the World's Top Sports Organizations (London: Profile Books, 2001)

182 Phil Jackson and Hugh Delehanty, Sacred Hoops: Spiritual Lessons of a Hardwood Warrior (New York: Hyperion, 1995). Quoted in Thomas Harvey, Bonita M. Drolet, and Douglas P. DeVore, Leading for Excellence: A Twelve Step Program to Student Achievement (Lanham, MD: Rowman & Littlefield Education, 2014), 92.

183 Elon Musk, 'The Mission of Tesla', Tesla UK (blog), 18 November 2013, https://www.tesla.com/en_GB/blog/mission-tesla

184 Innocent Drinks, 'The Innocent Promise: Tastes Good. Does Good.', Innocent, https://www.innocentdrinks.co.uk/the-innocent-promise (accessed 18 February 2021)

185 Anisa Khan, 'Innocent Drinks' (Prezi, 17 March 2011), https://prezi.com/4pelsh86lnl1/innocent-drinks/#:~:text=Innocent%20Drinks'%20purpose%20is%20to,good

186 Google, 'About Google, Our Culture & Company News', Google, https://about.google/ (accessed 18 February 2021)

187 Deloitte and Forbes Insights, 'Success Personified in the Fourth Industrial Revolution: Four Leadership Personas for an Era of Change and Uncertainty' (London: Deloitte, 2019), 5, https://www2.deloitte.com/content/dam/insights/us/articles/GLOB1948_Success-personified-4th-ind-rev/DI_Success-personified-fourth-industrial-revolution.pdf

188 Ibid.

189 United Nations Global Compact, 'The World's Largest Corporate Sustainability Initiative', UN Global Compact, https://www.unglobalcompact.org/what-is-gc; (accessed 18 February 2021) see also United Nations Global Compact, 'The Ten Principles of the UN Global Compact', UN Global Compact, https://www.unglobalcompact.org/what-is-gc/mission/principles (accessed 18 February 2021)

190 United Nations Global Compact, 'Our Mission', UN Global Compact, https://www.unglobalcompact.org/what-is-gc/mission/principles (accessed 18 February 2021)

191 United Nations Global Compact, 'What's the Commitment?', UN Global Compact, https://www.unglobalcompact.org/what-is-gc/mission/principles (accessed 18 February 2021)

192 Lise Kingo, 'Annual Letter from CEO & Executive Director of the UN Global Compact: A Year of Tipping Points', 16 January 2019, https://www.unglobalcompact.org/news/4422-01-16-2019

193 Nassim Nicholas Taleb, The Black Swan: The Impact of the Highly Improbable, 1st ed. (New York: Random House, 2007), xvii.

194 Rodney James Giblett, Black Swan Lake: Life of a Wetland (Bristol, UK: Intellect Books, 2013), 76–78.

195 Tim Low, 'Black Swan: The Impossible Bird', Australian Geographic, 11 July 2016, https://www.australiangeographic.com.au/topics/wildlife/2016/07/black-swan-the-impossible-bird/; VOC Historial Society, 'De Vlamingh', VOC Historical Society, http://www.vochistory.org.au/vlamingh.html (accessed 19 February 2021)

196 Taleb, The Black Swan, xvii.

197 Ibid., xviii.

198 The exact origin of this quote is unknown. Nevertheless, we feel comfortable attributing it to Jobs since, as Jason Aten notes in Inc., he made other similar statements which we can verify. See Jason Aten, 'This Is Steve Jobs' Most Controversial Legacy. It Is Also His Most Brilliant: When You Should Listen to Your Customers', Inc., 19 January 2021, https://www.inc.com/jason-aten/this-was-steve-jobs-most-controversial-legacy-it-was-also-his-most-brilliant.html

199 Henry Mason and Maria Isabel Reyes, Trend-Driven Innovation (Hoboken, NJ: John Wiley & Sons, 2015).

200 Raph Koster, A Theory of Fun for Game Design, 2nd ed. (O'Reilly Media: Sebastopol, CA, 2014), 40.

201 Koster, A Theory of Fun for Game Design.

202 Dictionary.com, 'Neurodiversity', in Dictionary.com (Oakland, CA: Dictionary.com), https://www.dictionary.com/browse/neurodiversity (accessed 23 March 2021)

203 World Health Organization and The World Bank, 'World Report on Disability' (Geneva: World Health Organization, 2011), 29, https://www.who.int/disabilities/world_report/2011/report.pdf

204 Doug McMillon, Walmart's CEO: 'We Are not as Diverse as We Want to Be', interview by David Rubenstein, TV interview, 14 July 2020, 0:46–0:57, https://www.bloomberg.com/news/articles/2020-07-13/walmart-s-mcmillon-we-are-not-as-diverse-as-we-want-to-be

205 Internal letter sent by John Donahoe to staff in June 2020. Quoted in Sara Germano, 'Nike Diversity Chief Leaves after Two Years in Role', Financial Times, 28 July 2020, https://www.ft.com/content/d294e62e-21e1-40af-8774-0ff354fbf4a5

206 NIKE, 'Purpose Moves Us: FY19 NIKE, Inc. Impact Report' (Beaverton, OR: NIKE, Inc.), 10, https://purpose.nike.com/fy19-nike-impact-report (accessed 19 February 2021)

207 Aimee Picchi, 'Goldman Sachs' New IPO Rule: No More All-White, Male Boards', CBS News, 24 January 2020, sec. Moneywatch, https://www.cbsnews.com/news/goldman-sachs-diversity-ipo-women-minorities-david-solomon-davos/

208 Elana Lyn Gross, 'The CEO Of Goldman Sachs Says The Bank Won't Take Companies Public Unless There Is At Least One "Diverse" Board

Member', Forbes, 23 January 2020, https://www.forbes.com/sites/elanagross/2020/01/23/the-ceo-of-goldman-sachs-says-it-wont-take-companies-public-unless-there-is-at-least-one-diverse-board-member/

209 Rocío Lorenzo et al., 'How Diverse Leadership Teams Boost Innovation' (Boston, MA: Boston Consulting Group, 23 January 2018), https://www.bcg.com/en-us/publications/2018/how-diverse-leadership-teams-boost-innovation

210 Vivian Hunt et al., 'Delivering through Diversity' (New York: McKinsey & Company, January 2018), 8, https://www.mckinsey.com/~/media/mckinsey/business%20functions/organization/our%20insights/delivering%20through%20diversity/delivering-through-diversity_full-report.ashx

211 Ibid., 10.

212 Speech delivered by John Amaechi at the Festival of Work 2020. Quoted in Francis Churchill, 'Learning Is Key to Addressing Racism, Amaechi Tells Festival of Work', People Management, 11 June 2020, https://www.peoplemanagement.co.uk/news/articles/learning-is-key-to-addressing-racism-issues-amaechi-tells-festival-of-work

213 Ibid.

214 EDUCBA, 'Does Swarming Technology Help Agile Teams Grow', EDUCBA (blog), https://www.educba.com/swarming-technology/ (accessed 19 February 2021)

215 See Jennifer Jordan and Michael Sorell, 'Why You Should Create a "Shadow Board" of Younger Employees', Harvard Business Review, 4 June 2019, https://hbr.org/2019/06/why-you-should-create-a-shadow-board-of-younger-employees

216 United Nations Population Division, 'World Population Prospects 2019 – Volume II: Demographic Profiles' (New York: United Nations, 2019), 5, https://population.un.org/wpp/Publications/Files/WPP2019_Volume-II-Demographic-Profiles.pdf

217 Wan He, Daniel Goodkind, and Paul Kowal, 'An Aging World: 2015 – International Population Reports' (Washington, DC: United States Census Bureau, March 2016), 3, https://www.census.gov/content/dam/Census/library/publications/2016/demo/p95-16-1.pdf

218 Ibid.

219 David Adams, 'Why Older People Will Need to Work Longer', ICAEW, https://www.icaew.com/groups-and-networks/communities/diversity-community/support-for-firms/why-older-people-will-need-to-work-longer (accessed 22 February 2021)

220 Adams, 'Why Older People Will Need to Work Longer'.

221 Shoko Oda, 'Silver Gifts to Centenarians Get Cheaper as Ranks Rise', The Japan Times, 17 September 2016, sec. Social Issues, https://www.japantimes.co.jp/news/2016/09/17/national/social-issues/number-japanese-centenarians-rises-silver-sake-cup-gifts-get-cheaper/

222 'Anniversary Messages', The Royal Family, https://www.royal.uk/anniversary-messages-0 (accessed 22 February 2021)

223 Oda, 'Silver Gifts to Centenarians Get Cheaper'.

224 John Bingham, 'Queen's "Birthday Card Team" Expands to Cope with Surge of 100-Year-Olds', The Telegraph, 25 September 2014, sec. News, https://www.telegraph.co.uk/news/health/elder/11121184/Queens-birthday-card-team-expands-to-cope-with-surge-of-100-year-olds.html

225 Kaare Christensen et al., 'Ageing Populations: The Challenges Ahead', The Lancet 374, no. 9696 (October 2009): 1197, https://doi.org/10.1016/S0140-6736(09)61460-4

226 Office for National Statistics, 'English Life Tables No. 17: 2010 to 2012', English Life Tables (Newport, Wales: Office for National Statistics, 1 September 2015), 5, https://www.ons.gov.uk/peoplepopulationandcommunity/birthsdeathsandmarriages/lifeexpectancies/bulletins/englishlifetablesno17/2015-09-01

227 Lynda Gratton and Andrew Scott, The 100-Year Life: Living and Working in an Age of Longevity (London: Bloomsbury Business, 2017).

228 Office for National Statistics, 'Living Longer and Old-Age Dependency – What Does the Future Hold?' (Newport, Wales: Office for National Statistics, 24 June 2019), 10, https://www.ons.gov.uk/peoplepopulationandcommunity/birthsdeathsandmarriages/ageing/articles/livinglongerandoldagedependencywhatdoesthefuturehold/2019-06-24 While the UK's retirement age is progressively rising to 67 in 2028, there is no way to break these figures down further to reflect this fact.

229 Adrian Gostick and Chester Elton, The Best Team Wins: The New Science of High Performance (New York: Simon & Schuster, 2018).

230 Ibid.

231 Dimock, 'Defining Generations'.

232 Ryan Pendell, 'Millennials Are Burning Out', Gallup (blog), 19 July 2018, https://www.gallup.com/workplace/237377/millennials-burning.aspx

233 Gallup, 'Gallup's Perspective on Employee Burnout: Causes and Cures' (Washington, DC: Gallup, 2020), 4, https://www.gallup.com/file/workplace/282659/Gallup%E2%80%99s%20Perspective%20on%20Employee%20Burnout%20Causes%20and%20Cures.pdf

234 Mo Gawdat, Solve for Happy: Engineer Your Path to Joy, Main Market ed. (London: Bluebird, 2019).

235 Ibid.

236 This quotation is often attributed to Plato, although, according to Gary Martin, this English saying predates the first translations of his Republic which include this sentence. See Gary Martin, 'The Meaning and Origin of the Expression: Necessity Is the Mother of Invention', The Phrase Finder, https://www.phrases.org.uk/meanings/necessityis-the-mother-of-invention.html (accessed 22 February 2021)

237 Kirsten Korosec, 'Starship Technologies Is Sending Its Autonomous Robots to More Cities as Demand for Contactless Delivery Rises', Tech Crunch, 9 April 2020, https://techcrunch.com/2020/04/09/starship-technologies-is-sending-its-autonomous-robots-to-more-cities-as-demand-for-contactless-delivery-rises/
238 Oliver Griffin and Nelson Bocanegra, 'Colombia's Rappi Trials Robots to Deliver Restaurant Food to Homes', Reuters, 17 April 2020, sec. Technology News, https://www.reuters.com/article/us-health-coronavirus-rappi-colombia-idUSKBN21Z3DF
239 BBC, 'Coronavirus: Robot Dog Enforces Social Distancing in Singapore Park', BBC News, 11 May 2020, sec. Technology, https://www.bbc.co.uk/news/av/technology-52619568
240 Ben Stevens, 'Lidl Launches WhatsApp Chatbot to Inform Customers When the Best Times to Shop Are', Charged, 12 May 2020, sec. Artificial Intelligence, https://www.chargedretail.co.uk/2020/05/12/lidl-launches-whatsapp-chatbot-to-inform-customers-when-the-best-times-to-shop-are/
241 Terry Clark, 'Diesel Introduces "HYPEROOM" 360 Selling Platform and Showroom', Retail Focus, 25 June 2020, https://www.retail-focus.co.uk/diesel-introduces-hyperoom-360-selling-platform-and-showroom/
242 Selecta, 'Selecta Introduces a Range of Convenient Hygiene and Safety Solutions to Help People Feel Safe When Returning to Work and While On-the-Go', Selecta (blog), 14 May 2020, https://www.selecta.com/media/Selecta-introduces-a-range-of-convenient-hygiene-and-safety-solutions/
243 Ann-Marie Corvin, 'Driving Audiences Back to the Big Screen', IBC, 2 June 2020, sec. Trends, https://www.ibc.org/trends/driving-audiences-back-to-the-big-screen/6037.article; Elissaveta M. Brandon, 'How the American Drive-In Staged a Comeback', Bloomberg, 4 September 2020, sec. CityLab, https://www.bloomberg.com/news/articles/2020-09-04/did-the-pandemic-save-the-drive-in-movie-theater
244 Tim Brown, Change by Design: How Design Thinking Transforms Organizations and Inspires Innovation, revised and updated ed. (New York: HarperCollins Publishers, 2019).
245 See e.g., Ted Burnham, 'How Einstein's "Best Friend at Work" Helped Him Revolutionize Physics', Avanoo (blog), https://www.avanoo.com/how-einsteins-best-friend-at-work-helped-himrevolutionize-physics/ (accessed 22 February 2021)
246 Steven Johnson, Where Good Ideas Come from: The Seven Patterns of Innovation (London: Penguin Books, 2011).
247 Ibid.
248 Getting Things Done®, 'About GTD®', Getting Things Done®, https://gettingthingsdone.com/about/ (accessed 1 March 2021)
249 Wang Tianyu, 'Employee Sharing Helps Companies Survive COVID-19', CGTN, 9 March 2020, sec. Biz Analysis, https://news.cgtn.com/

news/2020-03-09/Employee-sharing-helping-companies-get-through-COVID-19-OqvFZWc67m/index.html

250 Philip Tetlock and Dan Gardner, Superforecasting: The Art and Science of Prediction (London: Random House Books, 2016).

251 Michael Michalko, 'Creative Thinking and Leonardo Da Vinci', Think Jar Collective (blog), https://thinkjarcollective.com/articles/creative-thinking-leonardo-da-vinci/ (accessed 23 February 2021). See also Peter Fisk, 'What Is Innovation? Connecting the Dots, the Ones Other People Miss.', Peter Fisk (blog), 26 February 2016, https://www.peterfisk.com/2016/02/what-is-innovation-connecting-the-dots-the-ones-other-people-miss/

252 Fisk, 'What Is Innovation?'

253 Ibid.

254 Christensen Institute, 'Disruptive Innovation', Christensen Institute, https://www.christenseninstitute.org/key-concepts/disruptive-innovation-2/ (accessed 23 February 2021)

255 Clayton M. Christensen, Michael E. Raynor, and Rory McDonald, 'What Is Disruptive Innovation?', Harvard Business Review, December 2015, https://hbr.org/2015/12/what-is-disruptive-innovation.

256 Karen Dillon, 'What Clayton Christensen Taught Me', Harvard Business Review, 27 January 2020, https://hbr.org/2020/01/what-clayton-christensen-taught-me

257 Seth Godin, Stop Stealing Dreams (What Is School For?), free printable ed. (Hastings-on-Hudson, NY: Seth Godin), 47, https://seths.blog/wp-content/uploads/2019/05/stop-stealing-dreams6print.pdf (accessed 23 February 2021)

258 Ibid., 47–48.

259 Peter Fisk, Gamechangers: Are You Ready to Change the World? Creating Innovative Strategies for Business and Brands (Chichester, UK: John Wiley and Sons, 2015).

260 Ibid.

261 Ibid.

262 Ericka Blount Danois, 'Tarana Burke & the Future of the #MeToo Movement', Okayplayer, https://www.okayplayer.com/originals/tarana-burke-future-metoo.html (accessed 23 February 2021)

263 Faisal Hoque, Everything Connects: How to Transform and Lead in the Age of Creativity, Innovation, and Sustainability (New York: McGraw-Hill Education, 2014).

264 Aditya Shukla, 'Why Did Humans Evolve Pattern Recognition Abilities?', Cognition Today, 30 October 2020, https://cognitiontoday.com/why-did-humans-evolve-pattern-recognition-abilities/

265 Arkady Konovalov and Ian Krajbich, 'Neurocomputational Dynamics of Sequence Learning', Neuron 98, no. 6 (June 2018): 1282–93, https://doi.org/10.1016/j.neuron.2018.05.013; Jeff Grabmeier, 'This Is Your Brain Detecting Patterns: It Is Different from Other Kinds of Learning, Study

Shows', ScienceDaily, 31 May 2018, sec. Science News, https://www.sciencedaily.com/releases/2018/05/180531114642.htm
266 Jeff Grabmeier, 'This Is Your Brain Detecting Patterns: It Is Different from Other Kinds of Learning, Study Shows', ScienceDaily, 31 May 2018, sec. Science News, https://www.sciencedaily.com/releases/2018/05/180531114642.htm
267 Jeffrey Phillips, Relentless Innovation: What Works, What Doesn't – and What That Means for Your Business (New York: McGraw-Hill, 2012).
268 Jennifer Jordan and Michael Sorell, 'Why You Should Create a "Shadow Board" of Younger Employees', Harvard Business Review, 4 June 2019, https://hbr.org/2019/06/why-you-should-create-a-shadow-board-of-younger-employees
269 Ibid.
270 Ibid.
271 Ibid.
272 Ibid.
273 Ibid.
274 Ibid.
275 Ibid.
276 Ibid.
277 Jordan and Sorell, 'Why You Should Create a "Shadow Board" of Younger Employees'; Lucy Tobin, 'Shadow Boards: How Young Executives Are Running Corporates', London Evening Standard, 20 December 2019, sec. Business, https://www.standard.co.uk/business/shadow-boards-how-young-executives-are-running-corporates-a4318861.html
278 Lucy Tobin, 'Shadow Boards: How Young Executives Are Running Corporates', London Evening Standard, 20 December 2019, sec. Business, https://www.standard.co.uk/business/shadow-boards-how-young-executives-are-running-corporates-a4318861.html
279 Ibid.
280 Ibid.
281 Jordan and Sorell, 'Why You Should Create a "Shadow Board" of Younger Employees'.
282 Lucy Tobin, 'Shadow Boards: How Young Executives Are Running Corporates', London Evening Standard, 20 December 2019.
283 Jordan and Sorell, 'Why You Should Create a "Shadow Board" of Younger Employees'.
284 Jordan and Sorell, 'Why You Should Create a "Shadow Board" of Younger Employees'.
285 Thomas Armstrong, The Power of Neurodiversity: Unleashing the Advantages of Your Differently Wired Brain (Cambridge, MA: Da Capo Press, 2010).

286 Charlan Nemeth, In Defense of Troublemakers: The Power of Dissent in Life and Business (New York: Basic Books, 2018).
287 Ibid.
288 Charlan Jeanne Nemeth and Alexander O'Connor, 'Better than Individuals? Dissent and Group Creativity', in The Oxford Handbook of Group Creativity and Innovation (New York: Oxford University Press, 2019), 73–83.
289 Google, 'Guide: Understand Team Effectiveness', re:Work, https://rework.withgoogle.com/print/guides/5721312655835136/ (accessed 24 February 2021)
290 Harvard Business Review
291 Josh Bersin, 'New Research Shows "Heavy Learners" More Confident, Successful, and Happy at Work', LinkedIn (blog), 9 November 2018, https://www.linkedin.com/pulse/want-happy-work-spend-time-learning-josh-bersin/
292 Deloitte, 'The Deloitte Millennial Survey 2019: Societal Discord and Technological Transformation Create a "Generation Disrupted"' (London: Deloitte, 2019), 12, https://www2.deloitte.com/content/dam/Deloitte/global/Documents/About-Deloitte/deloitte-2019-millennial-survey.pdf
293 Udemy, '2018 Millennials at Work Report', Udemy in Depth (San Francisco: Udemy, 2018), 8, https://research.udemy.com/wp-content/uploads/2018/06/Udemy_2018_Measuring_Millennials_Report_20180618.pdf
294 Docebo, 'Fake It 'til You Make It? Understanding Employee Job Confidence and Know-How' (Toronto: Docebo, 17 January 2019), 4, https://cdn2.hubspot.net/hubfs/2016752/2019%20Q1%20JAN%20PR%20FITYMI%20Survey/Docebo-fake-it-til-you-make-it-survey.pdf
295 https://earthweb.com/how-many-google-searches-per-day/
296 Dan Schwabel, 'How to Use Storytelling as a Leadership Tool', Forbes, 13 August 2012, https://www.forbes.com/sites/danschawbel/2012/08/13/how-to-use-storytelling-as-a-leadership-tool
297 Dan Schwabel, 'How to Use Storytelling as a Leadership Tool', Forbes, 13 August 2012, https://www.forbes.com/sites/danschawbel/2012/08/13/how-to-use-storytelling-as-a-leadership-tool
298 Scott Goodson, Uprising: How to Build a Brand – and Change the World – by Sparking Cultural Movements (New York: McGraw-Hill, 2012).
299 Bruna Bezerra Lima, 'Behind Every Engagement There Is Always a Good Story', in Strategic Employee Communication, ed. Gail S. Thornton et al. (Cham, Switzerland: Springer International Publishing, 2019), 91–95.
300 Amy M. Boland, Catherine A. Haden, and Peter A. Ornstein, 'Boosting Children's Memory by Training Mothers in the Use of an Elaborative Conversational Style as an Event Unfolds', Journal of Cognition and Development 4, no. 1 (March 2003): 39–65, https://doi.org/10.1080/15248372.2003.9669682; The Pennsylvania State University, 'Developing Memory',

Penn State Extension, https://extension.psu.edu/programs/betterkidcare/early-care/tip-pages/all/developing-memory (accessed 26 February 2021)

301 Leo Wildrich, 'The Science of Storytelling: What Listening to a Story Does to Our Brains', Buffer (blog), 29 November 2012, https://buffer.com/resources/science-of-storytelling-why-telling-a-story-is-the-most-powerful-way-to-activate-our-brains/

302 Marshall Ganz, 'Worksheet: Telling Your Public Story – Self, Us, Now' (Welcoming Refugees, 2007), https://www.welcomingrefugees.org/sites/default/files/documents/resources/Public%20Story%20Worksheet07Ganz.pdf

303 Ellyn Shook, Mark Knickrehm, and Eva Sage-Gavin, 'Decoding Organizational DNA: Trust, Data and Unlocking Value in the Digital Workplace', Putting Trust to Work (Dublin: Accenture), 9, https://www.accenture.com/_acnmedia/Thought-Leadership-assets/PDF/Accenture-WF-Decoding-Organizational-DNA.pdf (accessed 24 February 2021)

304 The framework defines this as 'the cumulative knowledge, skills and abilities of an organisation's people and the impact on an organisation's long-term performance, as well as competitive advantage through optimising organisational outcomes'. Applicable to enterprises of all types and sizes, it provides guidelines on core HR areas such as organisational culture, recruitment and turnover, productivity, health and safety, and leadership. The goal is to help businesses create long-term and sustainable value through their people.

305 Roger Connors, Tom Smith, and Craig R. Hickman, The Oz Principle: Getting Results through Individual and Organizational Accountability, revised and updated ed. (New York: Portfolio, 2010).

306 Sonia Elks, 'Timeline: Greta Thunberg's Rise From Lone Protester to Nobel Favorite', Reuters, 3 October 2019, sec. Big Story 10, https://www.reuters.com/article/us-sweden-nobel-thunberg-timeline-idUSKBN1WI1RT; Natalie Gil, 'Greta Thunberg: The 16-Year-Old Climate Activist Who's Become a Global Celebrity', Refinery29, 15 March 2019, https://www.refinery29.com/en-gb/2019/03/227091/greta-thunberg-climate-strike-nobel-peace-prize

307 BBC, 'Greta Thunberg: Who Is She and What Does She Want?', BBC News, 28 February 2020, sec. Science & Environment, https://www.bbc.co.uk/news/world-europe-49918719

308 Ofcom, 'Children and Parents: Media Use and Attitudes Report 2019' (London: Ofcom, 4 February 2020), 20, https://www.ofcom.org.uk/__data/assets/pdf_file/0023/190616/children-media-use-attitudes-2019-report.pdf

309 Damian Carrington, 'School Climate Strikes: 1.4 Million People Took Part, Say Campaigners', The Guardian, 19 March 2019, sec. Environmental Activism, https://www.theguardian.com/environment/2019/mar/19/school-climate-strikes-more-than-1-million-took-part-say-campaigners-greta-thunberg

310 350.org, 'Over 4 Million People Strike for Climate Action', 350.org (blog), 20 September 2019, https://350.org/press-release/over-4-million-people-strike-for-climate-action/
311 BBC, 'Greta Thunberg: Who Is She and What Does She Want?', BBC News, 28 February 2020, sec. Science & Environment, https://www.bbc.co.uk/news/world-europe-49918719
312 Damian Carrington, 'Greta Thunberg Nominated for Nobel Peace Prize', The Guardian, 14 March 2019, sec. Greta Thunberg, https://www.theguardian.com/world/2019/mar/14/greta-thunberg-nominated-nobel-peace-prize.
313 Nelson Mandela, Long Walk to Freedom: The Autobiography of Nelson Mandela (London: Abacus, 2004).
314 Marshall Ganz, 'Leading Change: Leadership, Organization, and Social Movements', in Handbook of Leadership Theory and Practice: An HBS Centennial Colloquium on Advancing Leadership (Boston, MA: Harvard Business Press, 2010), 561.
315 Diana O'Brien and Jennifer Veenstra, 'Science of a Movement' (London: Deloitte, 2017), 3, https://www2.deloitte.com/content/dam/Deloitte/us/Documents/CMO/xc-science-of-movement-marketing.pdf
316 Greg Satell, Cascades: How to Create a Movement That Drives Transformational Change (New York: McGraw-Hill Education, 2019).
317 Malcolm Gladwell, The Tipping Point: How Little Things Can Make a Big Difference (London: Abacus, 2001).
318 Damon Centola, How Behavior Spreads: The Science of Complex Contagions, Princeton Analytical Sociology Series (Princeton, NJ: Princeton University Press, 2018).
319 University of Pennsylvania, 'Research Finds Tipping Point for Large-Scale Social Change', Annenberg School for Communication (blog), 7 June 2018, https://www.asc.upenn.edu/news-events/news/research-finds-tipping-point-large-scale-social-change
320 Damon Centola et al., 'Experimental Evidence for Tipping Points in Social Convention', Science 360, no. 6393 (8 June 2018): 1118, https://doi.org/10.1126/science.aas8827
321 Ibid.

Printed in Great Britain
by Amazon

38142009R00137